when *faith*

is not enough

when *faith*

is not enough

kelly james clark

William B. Eerdmans Publishing Company
Grand Rapids, Michigan / Cambridge, U.K.

© 1997 Wm. B. Eerdmans Publishing Co.
255 Jefferson Ave. S.E., Grand Rapids, Michigan 49503 /
P.O. Box 163, Cambridge CB3 9PU U.K.

Printed in the United States of America

02 01 00 99 98 97   7 6 5 4 3 2 1

Library of Congress Cataloging-in-Publication Data

Clark, Kelly James, 1956-   .
    When faith is not enough / Kelly James Clark.
        p.   cm.
    Includes bibliographical references.
    ISBN 0-8028-4354-9 (alk. paper)
    1. Faith.   I. Title.
    BT771.2.C565   1997
    248.8′6—dc21   97-17758
                                CIP
                                                    ?

Unless otherwise noted, Scripture quotations are from the New Revised Standard Version of the Bible, copyright © by the Division of Christian Education of the National Council of the Churches of Christ in the U.S.A., and used by permission.

to my children,

will, emily, and evan:

moments of light

Contents

Part II. Searching for My Self

Don't Skip This!

Several years ago I took a trip to Wyoming to climb the Grand Teton mountain. Just before embarking on the long hike up the canyon, I learned that someone had died in the canyon the day before. The person who died had come to the mountains unprepared — no rope, no ice axe, no protective clothing. He slipped while walking across one of the canyon's spectacular hanging snow fields. Thinking himself relatively secure, he had simply taken one false step. Perhaps the warming snow gave way underneath his sneakers. I can imagine him being awed at his magnificent surroundings and wandering off the beaten path. There he is shooting down a steep snow slope, something he has never experienced before in his life. Unaware of the danger, he starts hooting in delight like a child on his first toboggan ride. His exultation gradually changes into fear as he realizes that his speed is rapidly increasing and that it is impossible to stop. His friends cringe at his screams of terror as he plummets out of their sight to his death.

The hiker's initial reaction disguised the genuine danger he was in. Perhaps it would have been better for him to remain in blissful ignorance right up to his unexpected end. The realization of a disastrous end robbed the snowslide of any delight, and his awareness of an immediately ensuing death produced only fear. If only he could have persuaded himself that he was on a long toboggan ride. But he could not. As death approached, the man surely doubted the wisdom of taking that path. Too late, his regrets.

It may be odd to begin a book with such a grim story, but the story as I've told it illustrates the two themes of this book. We have all made commitments about ultimate reality — whether or not there is a God and how that God is best approached — and we have all made judgments about how best to attain happiness in this life. As we shoot ever more rapidly toward death, we begin to wonder whether or not we have chosen the right path. Will our path lead to true knowledge of self and God? Are we being directed towards happiness, genuine human fulfillment, or are we plummeting towards an insignificant, meaningless existence that terminates in the grave? If so, wouldn't it be better just to live a drugged existence, blissfully unaware of both our plight and our destiny? Doubt and death, God and self, happiness or insignificance, guilt or grace — these fundamental human concerns are deeply intertwined and connect with our heart's deepest longings. We don't want to take the wrong path on any of these matters. We are getting closer to the end, progressing much more rapidly than at the beginning, and we want to be sure that we are heading in the right direction toward self, God, happiness, and grace.

You have resisted the temptation to skip the introduction and get right into the meat of this book. I'd like to set the stage for the two parts of this book. Part I is a discussion of the oft-ignored topic of doubt. I believe readers will learn more about authentic faith by reflecting on doubt and will also learn more about their own religious beliefs and uncertainties. Part II is a reflection on the meaning of life. This is, again, a topic seldom discussed, except perhaps jokingly, but one that is often deeply felt. Doubt and the meaning of life: these are issues often ignored, denied, repressed, and dismissed, but they are felt.

The central topic of this book is faith: how to have faith in the midst of our doubts; how faith alone synthesizes the disparate elements of our self — finite and infinite, wicked and good, necessary and free, temporal and eternal, body and spirit — into a meaningful whole. We have doubts, to be sure. But the benefits of faith are so great — only through faith can we live an authentic, happy, and fulfilled life — that the struggles of life and belief are worth the effort.

Part I: the shadow of a doubt

The first half of the book is not triumphal. It won't resolve everything to everyone's satisfaction, and it doesn't offer pat answers. It does what it says it is going to do — take doubt (and doubters) seriously. It helps the reader to understand faith in a deeper way, presents a case for the existence of God, offers hope for understanding the problem of God and human suffering, suggests positive ways for dealing with doubt, and affirms the excitement of embracing the adventure of life. It does this knowing that reasonable people will say, "Yes, but" and it allows people their "buts."

How should we understand faith in the midst of our ambiguous, ambivalent, and suffering world? We have moments of light when God seems clearly evident and moments of darkness when we sense God's hiddenness or absence. How do we reconcile these contradictory impulses in our believing nature? The chapters in this part of the book explore faith and doubt through personal experience, through the stories of Abraham and Job, and through the insights of the great Christian philosopher, Søren Kierkegaard.

Part II: searching for my self

What is the meaning of life? No other question is as likely to raise eyebrows and elicit snickers as this. Nevertheless, most people feel the force of the question — and their lack of answers — at some time in their lives. People feel disheartened, lost, and alone. The fragile grip we have on life is broken by suffering, monotony, and reflection. We want our lives to count but feel insignificant. We desire fame and honor but seem forgotten and ignored. Wishing for significant human relationships, we often feel alienated and unable to communicate. And wanting to live a worthy life, we feel shame. The seriousness of these issues breaks through the jocularity, and the question forces itself upon us: does my life have any meaning?

Christians blithely claim that life has meaning but seldom reflect on how faith in God makes life meaningful. Part II of this book explores our most profound human attempts to find meaning and happiness and explains why they invariably lead to despair and brokenness. The central theme of this section is the attempt to create a self of abiding value. We are creatures, not creators, so our attempts to create a self are doomed to failure. Our true self is found through faith in God. How does God unite the disparate elements of our lives into a meaningful and enduring whole?

Although the initial chapters in Part II are rather gloomy, overall this section is positive and engaging. Its inspiration is again the work of Kierkegaard as well as the atheistic existentialists who followed him. It offers philosophical reflection on fundamental human needs — for significance, security, and the desire to know and be known. It draws on poetry, literature, film, music, and Scripture to illuminate the human quest for self-understanding, ultimate significance, and happiness. The adventure of faith, I shall argue, is worth the effort because only through faith in God can our deepest needs be satisfied — our need to find our self, to live a fulfilled life, to feel secure, to redeem time, and to be forgiven.

the ride

When my son Will was three years old, we took a trip to Disney World. With his younger sister we took the baby rides, but Will was ready for something wilder. So we waited in the interminably long line for the roller coaster ride through a gold mine. As we approached the coasters, we could hear the squeaking of the metal and the squealing of the passengers. "What's all that noise, Daddy?" "Where are all those screams coming from?" "Why are they screaming, Daddy?" "Yeah, I think I still want to go on this ride." Will's delight and terror grew as we sat down and peered into the darkness into which we would soon fly. "Where does this thing go, Daddy?" On came the seat belts. I held him close, assured him of a safe and fun ride, and then off we went!

The journey was tame for a hardcore coaster rider like me, but it was pure excitement for a young boy. The ride was filled with fits and starts; we jerked into motion, around corners, down unseen hills, and came to a stop to view facades of miners. "Ohhhhh, nooooo!" "Why are we going so fast?" We hit bumps hard, and the drops were swift and startling. There were close calls as we nearly bashed other cars and near misses as it seemed we would crash into the walls. I held him close to me and looked into his anxious, thrilled face. I had to assure him that we would have a safe trip and a happy ending. "Is it OK if I hold onto your hand?" "Hang on, Daddy!"

The Disney engineers and workers had conspired to design and construct a safe yet exhilarating ride. We were never in any real danger. And I was there to communicate my love and concern. Will, confident that we wouldn't crash and die, enjoyed the ride. All in all, it was a rollicking and harrowing journey for a three-year-old. The ride was made tolerable, in part, by my continual assurance that everything would be all right. "That was fun, Daddy. Do you want to go again?"

This book will take the reader on a similar rollicking and harrowing journey. For it tracks the journey through faith and doubt, which is fraught with emotional and intellectual ups and downs. This ride will take us from light to darkness, from high to low, from peace to suffering, and from comfort to anxiety and back again to tranquillity. Our ultimate destination is not at all clear. Our track will be dialectical — from moments of light we will shift into moments of darkness. We will find some solace when rediscovering the radical nature of faith, but we will be forced back into the dim world of human misery. Finally, we will notice some glad glimmers of hope and find some concluding yet provisional resolutions of living with doubt, guilt, and death.

Fits and starts, sudden stops, near misses, crashes and bashes, unseen drops and walls, and no end in sight. I would like to assure the reader, as I could my son, that everyone will have a safe trip and a happy ending. But I cannot. This ride is dangerous, the human contents of the coaster are often spilled, and we can't see our destination. But life isn't optional. We must ride. So hang on!

part I

The Shadow of a Doubt

One must know when it is right to doubt,
to affirm, to submit.

Pascal, *Pensées*

chapter 1

Inside the
Darkness

Fact is sonny, I've always had notions of my own concerning young David's harp. A gifted lad, to be sure, but not all his strumming kept him clear of mortal sin. Of course I know our poor dear old-fashioned scribblers, with their tuppeny Lives of the Saints, take it for granted that a fellow can find safety in transports of ecstasy, that he curls himself up all snug and safe as though he were in Abraham's bosom? Safe? . . . Oh, I grant you there are times when it's as simple as pie to attain such heights. God sweeps you up. The real snag is to stick there, and know how to get down again — when you can't hold on any longer. . . .

Georges Bernanos, *Diary of a Country Priest*

The Bible knows of God's hiding His face, of times when the contact between Heaven and earth seems to be interrupted. God seems to withdraw Himself utterly from the earth and no longer to participate in its existence. The space of history is then full of noise, but as it were, empty of divine breath. For one who believes in the living God, who knows about Him, and is fated to spend his life in a time of His hiddenness, it is very difficult to live.

Martin Buber, "The Dialogue between Heaven and Earth"

The Sea of Faith,
Was once, too, at the full, and round earth's shore
Lay like the folds of a bright girdle furl'd.
But now I only hear
Its melancholy, long, withdrawing roar,
Retreating, to the breath
Of the night-winds, down the vast edges drear
And naked shingles of the world.

Ah, love, let us be true
To one another! for the world, which seems
To lie before us like a land of dreams,
So various, so beautiful, so new,
Hath really neither joy, nor love, nor light,
Nor certitude, nor peace, nor help for pain;
And we are here as on a darkling plain
Swept with confus'd alarms of struggle and flight,
Where ignorant armies clash by night.

Matthew Arnold, *Dover Beach*

ooooo

I went hiking many years ago with a well-known mountain guide. We took a lunch break in a wondrous canyon, surrounded on all sides by magnificent wildflowers in full bloom. I had recently read that one of America's most famous climbers, a pioneer of many extreme ascents, professed to be a Christian. Since my guide knew this famous climber, I asked him about the circumstances surrounding the climber's conversion. He sneered that the famous climber had joined the "cargo cult." Since I was unfamiliar with this exotic sounding cult, I asked him to explain.

During World War II, the guide explained, the United States military mistakenly but periodically parachuted supplies to a group of natives living on a small island in the South Pacific (they knew nothing of wars or rumors of wars). The supplies included food items, for which they were extremely grateful. I am told they grew especially fond of canned peaches. Once a week they looked to the eastern skies for the anticipated return of the cargo plane, which would miraculously deliver their tin bounty. They looked upon these deliveries as a sign of favor with the gods. When the war ended, however, the deliveries ceased. Nevertheless, the natives regularly gathered at the appointed time to await their sign of the gods' favor.

According to my guide, becoming a Christian is tantamount to joining the cargo cult—one must be misinformed and credulous while waiting for a messenger from a self-created God. We have all had the fear of joining the cargo cult. Although we have made religious commitments, we are often anxious that we may await his return as the natives awaited the return of the cargo planes—benighted and misinformed.

the shadow of a doubt

Authentic Christian faith is at once compelling and disputable. We live in a post-modern and post-Christian world, where certainty is an illusion and where many hold our deepest commitments in suspicion. For those outside of a religious community, faith seems monumentally absurd and to some, morally perverse. That many people whom we respect find the Christian faith intellectually deficient is a source of consternation. The world no longer seems solidly Christian. We are making our way through shadows of gray. We form our beliefs in a wilderness of darkness. Doubts seem inevitable.

What does it mean to be an authentic religious believer when we are called to have a sure and certain faith but see our present believing reality plagued with ambiguity and doubt? Our traditional confessions of faith are a reproach when we mouth words that do not resonate deeply within our hearts. The classical creeds and confessions seem to give witness to a distant era when belief was somehow easier. We are left to find our way in this world with little guidance and, so it often seems, with little honesty from our religious leaders. Doubt is the secret sin buried deep within our souls. We are all afraid to touch it, to unloose the monster. But authentic Christian belief demands that we uncover it, name it, understand it, and make our peace with it. We must learn to live as sincere believers in an age of unbelief— honestly acknowledging the enemy that lies within. This chapter will consider the major sources of doubt and their recent expressions.

the hiddenness of God

In *The Diary of a Country Priest* by Georges Bernanos there is a remarkable interchange between a young country priest and a wizened priest near his parish. The ancient cleric is more worldly wise than his younger counterpart and has clearly struggled his whole life with matters of faith and doubt. While conceding the ease of belief that attends those privileged mortals who catch momentary glimpses of the divine—"curl[ed] up all snug and safe as though he were in Abraham's bosom"—he is also aware of the difficulties that attend ordinary believers on the descent from Mt. Carmel: "The real snag is to stick there, and know how to get down again—when you can't hold on any longer...."[1] It's easy to believe during a moving worship service, upon hearing a powerful sermon, or while watching the sun set during a retreat. But how are we to believe when our children are squawking, our finances are a mess, and a beautiful and talented teenager in our church suddenly dies in her sleep?

Deus absconditus—the hidden God. While we long for assurance of God's presence, God often seems distant, even nonexistent. Our prayers go unanswered. Worship feels rote and meaningless. Suffering

1. Georges Bernanos, *The Diary of a Country Priest* (New York: Macmillan, 1948), 14.

seems senseless and gratuitous. God's hiddenness is not without biblical witness. Job, in the midst of his sufferings, calls out: "Oh that I knew where I might find him, that I might come even to his dwelling! . . . If I go forward, he is not there; or backward, I cannot perceive him" (Job 23:3-4, NRSV).

Pascal writes: "Truly, thou art a hidden God." The hiddenness of God is a topic seldom discussed by Christians, but it is a prime source of our anxiety. In it are rooted the problems of religious doubt, human suffering, and the meaning of life. If God were tangible, or if easily identifiable signs of his existence confronted us everywhere, we would rest in a sublime and confident faith. But so often we look for God and, like Job, discover that he is not there. We are left to find our way in a world dimmed by sin and suffering.

God's silence

Human suffering would be infinitely more bearable if we knew the purposes it served, but we do not. Some suffering seems to have no point except to dehumanize us. God's hiddenness while we suffer is particularly vexing—just when he is most needed, he seems most absent. Some people, of course, find God an ever present help in time of need. Others, including many biblical writers, hear only silence in their sufferings. While we long for the faith of the triumphant, who cling to God even in the silence, our suffering is often exacerbated by God's very hiddenness. Our physical and emotional pains are magnified by God's refusal to answer our "Why?" We cry out with the suffering Psalmist, "O God, do not keep silence; do not hold your peace or be still, O God!" (83:1).

The silence of God is a recurring theme in the so-called lament Psalms. Nearly half of the Psalms are lamentations of God's apparent abandonment of his people. They are cries of complaint to a God who seems indifferent to Israel's wretched plight. These Psalms are written out of human misery by people who wonder whether God is faithful or good. Is God really on the side of justice? Why do the wicked prosper and the righteous perish? Where is God in the midst of all this? The lament Psalms are honest expressions of despair concerning God's silence in the midst of human suffering. They are often desperate attempts to remind God of his promises, to persuade him of the worthiness of their cause, and to cajole him into action. They are expressions of doubt typically followed by affirmations of faith.

> How long, O LORD? Will you forget me forever?
>   How long will you hide your face from me?
> How long must I bear pain in my soul
>   and have sorrow in my heart all day long?
>   How long shall my enemy be exalted over me?
>
> Consider and answer, O LORD my God.
>   Give light to my eyes, or I will sleep the sleep of death,
> and my enemy will say, "I have prevailed";
>   my foes will rejoice because I am shaken.
>
> But I trusted in your steadfast love;
>   my heart shall rejoice in your salvation.
> I will sing to the LORD,
>   because he has dealt bountifully with me.
>
> Psalm 13

The meaning of life is veiled within the cloak of human ignorance. We seem constitutionally incapable of attaining lasting peace and happiness. Our lives are a frantic scramble from one momentary pleasure (or avoidance of pain) to the next, as we search for fulfillment of our human potential. We are sailing, so often it seems, in a ship on a vast sea with neither pilot nor destination, hoping for a time when the seas are sufficiently calm to grant us a moment's reprieve. Most of us, however, have developed habits that deaden us to these ultimate issues. When these issues are resurrected — by a mid-life crisis, for example, or by losing a job or a spouse or a child — we are desperate for divine guidance. Yet we often discover the divine absence. Why do God's answers seem enigmatic or unattainable?

Why, when our suffering seems capricious and our lives mean-ingless, do the churches only read and sing the happy Psalms? Why don't we incorporate honest expressions of doubt and anguish into our modern worship? Why don't we proclaim from our pulpits and pronounce from our pews exactly what we often feel — that God has ignored us? Psalm 88 expresses deep anguish at God's absence and does not resolve itself with even a feeble affirmation of faith. Consider the last six verses:

> But I cry to you for help, O LORD;
>> in the morning my prayer comes before you.
> Why, O LORD, do you reject me
>> and hide your face from me?
>
> From my youth I have been afflicted and close to death;
>> I have suffered your terrors and am in despair.
> Your wrath has swept over me;
>> your terrors have destroyed me.
> All day long they surround me like a flood;
>> they have completely engulfed me.
> You have taken my companions and loved ones from me;
>> the darkness is my closest friend.
>>> Psalm 88:13-18, NIV

Christians, of all people, should be honest about their plight, but they are curiously silent on the topic of honest and sincere doubt. It is, for many, an unspeakable sin. We should heed the comment of Leslie Stephen: "Why, when no honest man will deny in private that every ultimate problem is wrapped in the profoundest mystery, do honest men proclaim in pulpits that unhesitating certainty is the duty of the most foolish and ignorant? Is it not a spectacle to make the angels laugh?"[2]

the tide of history

We live in an unbelieving and increasingly pluralist generation, and we are products of our culture, whether we want to be or not. Philosopher Steven Cahn considers the status of modern atheism through a character in Tom Stoppard's play *Jumpers:* "Well, the tide is running his way, and it is a tide which has turned only once in human history. . . . There is presumably a calendar date — a moment — when the onus of proof passed from the atheist to the believer, when, quite suddenly, secretly, the noes had it."[3] Cahn believes that this calendar date coincides with the publication in 1779 of David Hume's powerful critique of arguments for the existence of God, *Dialogues Concerning Natural Religion.* While his dating of the turning point may be debated, there has been a decisive turn towards unbelief in Western culture (at least among intellectuals); the "noes" have it.

Each advance in science, declares the modern atheist, signals just another retreat for religious belief. As knowledge in science increases, the necessity for a divine architect and unmoved mover decreases. Nature, moved by internal forces such as inertia and natural selection, no longer needs Supernature to account for it. According to the scientific high priests of our culture, the battles fought by Copernicus, Galileo, Newton, and especially Darwin have spelled decisive defeat for belief in God. Richard Dawkins, professor of biology at Oxford

2. Leslie Stephen, *An Agnostic's Apology and Other Essays* (New York: Putnam's Sons, 1893), 39.

3. Steven Cahn, "The Challenge of Hume's *Dialogue," Newsletter on Teaching Philosophy* 88 (1988): 63.

University, has recently written, "Darwin made it possible to be an intellectually fulfilled atheist."[4] While there is no logical connection between accepting evolutionary theory and atheism, there are few who have not felt an awkward tension between science and religion.

In his poem *Dover Beach*, which is subtitled *The Eternal Note of Sadness*, Matthew Arnold writes of the retreat of faith and the spread of doubt in his generation. For Arnold this lack of faith is no cause for celebration; the world now lacks a loving and redeeming center to reconcile all things. There is now, he writes elsewhere, no place to lay one's head. Where people once heard the voice of God crashing in on the waves, now Arnold hears only silence. The sea of faith is no longer "at the full," and its loss is a reason for melancholy. Long gone are the days of Arnold, when the retreat of faith was a source of lament. We must find our way, these days, in a culture only too eager to embrace life in the wake of lost faith.

perils of pluralism

Many Christians also find themselves doubting that they have committed themselves to the one true God. This doubt comes in many forms. Some may feel that, had they not been born of Christian parents in the West — in "one nation under God" (the God of Abraham, Isaac, and Jacob) — they might have grown up Muslim, Buddhist, Taoist, or Hindu. Is it merely a fluke of birth that makes Christianity seem true and Jesus real? Is one's religious identity merely an accident of history or geography, like having a southern accent? We grow into accents; do we simply grow into religious belief? Our Judeo-Christian culture prepares us to prefer monotheism, rising gods, forgiveness and sanctification, baptism and biblical ethics. Are we Christians simply because of our sociocultural upbringing?

4. Richard Dawkins, *The Blind Watchmaker* (New York: Norton, 1986), 6.

In a famous article, H. L. Mencken presents a long, sobering list of gods that no longer commend belief. A small sample of his list includes such notables as Huitzilopochtli, Quetzalcoatl, Tialoc, Centeotl, Mixcoatl, Mullo, Tarves, Damona, Esus, Silvana, Ogmios, Sutekh, Resheph, Ashtoreth, Nebo, Melek, Addu, Osiris, Baal, Morrigu, Mulu-hursang, Ops, Vesta, Zagaga, Llaw Gyffes, Mu-ul-il, Qarradu, and Merodach. He concludes: "You may think that I spoof. That I invent the names. I do not. Ask the rector to lend you any good treatise on comparative religion: You will find them all listed. They were gods of the highest standing and dignity—gods of civilized people—worshiped and believed in by millions. All were theoretically omnipotent, omniscient, and immortal. And all are dead."[5]

While Mencken refrains from drawing any conclusions, he surely means to cast doubt on the existence of any gods and on the assurance of commitment to the one, true god. How likely is it that we are right in our religious convictions and everyone else is wrong? At times, Christians doubt that they have gotten religious matters right—that their god alone of these thousands of dead gods is alive and well and worthy of adoration.

incarnations, etc.

Religious doubts run deeper than mere reflection on the sociohistorical background of one's beliefs. Christian belief itself is beset with sources of doubt. The very notion of an incarnation is improbable, if not impossible. How could a being be both fully God and fully man? Aren't these two categories mutually exclusive? Can a being be both omnipotent and a baby? Can a being be both utterly independent and yet need his mama for sustenance? Christian belief would be vastly easier if the early Church had not adopted the ambitious doctrine

---

5. H. L. Mencken, *A Mencken Chrestomathy* (New York: Knopf, 1922), 95-99.

that Jesus was fully god and fully man. Part god and part human maybe, but 100 percent of both divinity and humanity creates a huge obstacle to belief. Maybe it was easier to embrace contradictions or paradoxes in ancient times.

What else are Christians expected to believe? For starters, they are supposed to believe that two thousand years ago an itinerant Jewish preacher from an obscure village in a tiny and insignificant country declared that the kingdom of God was at hand. He was born of a virgin who was impregnated by God himself. He worked wonders and miracles, such as giving sight to the blind, turning water into wine, and calming the seas. He claimed to be God in the flesh and demanded that all people believe in him and eat his flesh in order to be saved. He predicted that he would die, rise again in three days, and ascend to heaven. He promised to return for the final judgment, when all people would be consigned to eternal bliss or to eternal punishment. He entrusted these teachings to a small band of unlikely followers and charged them with disseminating his message to the world. He was captured by the religious authorities in Jerusalem. After a hasty and bizarre trial, he was sentenced, crucified, and buried in a tomb. On the third day, he rose from the dead as he predicted he would. His resurrection empowered his disheartened followers and led to the foundation of the Church. The only documents that report these astonishing claims were written by followers intent on drawing people to this new religion of which they would be leaders.

And what is at stake in this new religion? Nothing less than one's eternal destiny. The exclusive right to salvation is claimed by Jesus, and refusal to accept these beliefs results in eternal damnation. The stakes could not be higher. We are gambling our eternal destiny on poorly attested reports of astonishing items for belief. Is it fair to make one's hope of salvation rest on such a frail reed? Why, when so much is at stake, is the source of confidence so fragile?

the demand for evidence

To raise the problem of evidence, consider the following example. Suppose you are trying to decide which way to vote in a presidential election. Would it be reasonable for you to vote Republican because your parents are Republican or because the community in which you were raised is largely Republican? What would make your vote for the Republican candidate *reasonable?* You would have to examine the issues, watch the debates, observe how the candidates behave under pressure, and see how they respond to contrary positions. Then you would have to make your best judgment. Only then would your vote be reasonable. People cast votes for a variety of reasons, but careful consideration of the evidence is the rational basis on which to vote. Why is it important to examine the evidence when voting for the President of the United States? Because the stakes are so high. *The higher the stakes, the greater the demand for evidence.* If it is true that high stakes create a greater demand for evidence, then we ought to have the greatest demand for evidence of our Christian beliefs. Yet we are typically satisfied with so little. The stakes could not be higher — eternal bliss or eternal torment — so the demand for evidence seems maximal.

Many preachers proclaim with so much verbosity that Christian beliefs are easily attained and maintained. To those flagging in belief, they simply reassert these troublesome beliefs, only louder. They believe that shrill and repetitive assertion passes for rational persuasion. They proclaim as crystal clear an enigma wrapped in obscurity. They do not understand how anyone could refuse what seems to them so obvious. They are eager to deny what neither Jesus' followers nor Jesus himself denied: "This teaching is difficult; who can accept it?" (John 6:60).

15

inside the darkness

A coal mine is hushed and dark like a tomb. Its long passageways extend like the tentacles of an octopus grasping for bits of coal through a vast sea of dirt. When miners enter this silent world, the curtain closes on the world of light and sound. The birds don't chirp, leaves don't rustle in the wind, the sun's rays are blocked by flinty soil, and fresh air can't enter. Down, down the miners travel, first into the cool, then into the cold, and then into the hellish heat. The miners listen intently for the cracking of the roof to sound a warning of impending disaster. Within seconds or minutes, or maybe hours, or perhaps even days, the cracking ceases and the roof collapses.

Miners break up rock with dynamite. The smoke and dust are often so thick that the miners can't see anything; if they hear a crack, they don't know which way to go. They listen and look for the scuffling of mine rats. Due to the constricting of their dens and passageways, the rats sense the settling that precedes a cave-in. As soon as the rats attempt to exit the mine, the workers quickly follow. Miners spurn the use of earplugs; they want to hear the warnings of danger. With the advent of new technology, however, comes a new danger: machinery so noisy that miners can't hear the ceilings cracking.

Haulage accidents pose another danger: you can get crushed between two cars or run over by a car. Long ago workers entered mine shafts in baskets with a counterweight basket of coal rising alongside. Occasionally the counterweight would bang the side of the mine, sway toward the other basket, and then collide with the basket of people, causing them to plummet to their death.

Explosions pose yet another threat. The most fortunate are killed instantly. Others survive the blast but suffocate in the spreading carbon monoxide. Some live for weeks or months behind blocked exits — perhaps to be rescued, perhaps to starve to death. Fire in the mines can travel at a speed of five thousand miles per hour. If the flames

16

don't get you, the dust will. A whirlpool of fire consumes everything in its path. The dust itself is explosive. Add to it a wee bit of gas, and it becomes deadly. Loaded cars weighing tons could be thrown from their tracks.

Miners used to use birds for a warning, because birds are more sensitive than humans to poisonous gas. Many miners die trying to rescue their trapped friends. A crack in the wall can unleash a pocket of methane gas. One spark and the whole mine can blow up. Miners used to light their way with candles. But the deeper and more gaseous the mines, the more dangerous this becomes. Safety lamps were introduced, but all that did was to allow miners to penetrate deeper into a pocket of gas before it exploded.

In 1869 a fire swept through a mine in which 179 men and boys were trapped. They feverishly built a barricade to hold back the fumes and smoke. The rescue party arrived too late and found a father and his son locked in one another's arms; some were kneeling in prayer.

So many passageways, so many wrong ways to go, so many ways to die, and so little light. So we listen to the cracks, follow the fleeing footsteps of rats, watch for gasping pigeons, live in fear, cling to one another, kneel in prayer, and search for glimpses of light.

chapter 2

Moments
of Light

The world's a school, where (in a general story)
God always reads dumb lectures of his glory:
A pair of stairs, whereby our mounting soul
Ascends by steps above the archèd pole:
A sumptuous hall, where God (on every side)
His wealthy shop of wonders opens wide:
A bridge, whereby we may pass o'er (at ease),
Of sacred secrets the broad boundless seas.

. . . . . .

The world's a book in folio, printed all
With God's great works in letters capital:
Each creature is a page; and each effect
A fair character, void of all defect.
But, as young truants, toying in the schools,
Instead of learning, learn to play the fools:
We gaze but on the babies and the cover,
The gawdy flowers, and edges gilded over;
And never farther for our lesson look
Within the volume of this various book;
Where learned nature rudest ones instructs,
That, by his wisdom, God the world conducts.

. . . . . .

But he that wears the spectacles of faith,
Sees through the spheres, above the highest height:
He comprehends the Arch-mover of all motions
And reads (though running) all these needful notions.

Du Bartas, *Divine Weeks and Works*

I had always vaguely felt facts to be miracles in the sense that they
are wonderful: now I began to think them miracles in the stricter
sense that they were *wilful*. I mean that they were, or might be,

repeated exercises of some will. In short, I had always believed that the world involved magic: now I thought that perhaps it involved a magician. And this pointed to a profound emotion always present and sub-conscious; that this world of ours has some purpose; and if there is a purpose, there is a person. I had always felt life first as a story: and if there is a story there is a story-teller.

G. K. Chesterton, *Orthodoxy*

ooooo

I n the smile of a child, at the birth of a baby, in the beauty of a sunset, in the majesty of mountains, in the joy of friendship — in all these we see the face of God. Irresistibly the conviction wells up within: there must be a God. For how could we have the heavens and the earth and all they contain? How could there be life and breath and goodness and beauty? This chapter explores our moments of light, glimpses of God in people and in nature.

moment of grace

In 1987 I was traveling in Europe with a group of college students. Most of the students were at best art likers, not lovers, and initially they felt compelled to visit art museums because they felt some pressure from me to appreciate all aspects of European culture. To my surprise, they took to this challenge with gusto. In the Wallraf Richartz Museum, Cologne, Germany, several students excitedly approached me and declared that there was a beautiful painting that I must see. I followed them into the appropriate room and faced a marvelous painting that stretched from the floor to the ceiling, Salvador Dali's *The Station of Perpignan*.

Its great size made it difficult to discern any details, but gradually the entire painting came into focus. The outer sections were clear — powerful images of poor, working-class people — and the top contained a train with a man floating above it. Four rays of light streamed from the center into the corners, but the faint image in the center was hard to make out. It was almost as if Dali had created a painting that defied a central focal point; yet slowly the center became clear. The brightest colors in the painting were just below the center — the reds and blacks from which a bleeding slash of human flesh was painted.

As I focused on the bleeding slash, the rest of the picture slowly emerged. The slash was Christ's side, pierced by the soldier's spear. The dramatic center was the crucifixion of Christ. The focus of the center was Christ's wound, and it engendered powerful feelings of the passion of Christ. The long arms of the suffering Christ reached out to embrace not only the peasants in the painting but all who entered the room. I don't know what Dali intended to communicate in this surrealistic scene, but I do know how I felt when I viewed it. I felt, very powerfully, that Christ's arms were reaching out to embrace *me*, that Christ had died for *me*.

surprised by humility

After I graduated from high school in 1974, I took a summer job as a night-shift janitor in a hospital. Although I was "just a janitor," I kept my pride intact by reminding myself that I was headed for college while my fellow employees were not. I maintained my self-worth, in part, by looking down on them. One of the employees, Leon, befriended me. He was a kindly, graying, fifty-year-old African-American who hauled trash in his rusty pickup truck by day and worked as a janitor by night. By his hard work he was able to support his family, although it was unclear to me when he slept or how he was able to spend time with them!

For the evening meal break, I would sit alone and read. I prided myself on being responsible with my time. The professional janitors sat together and enjoyed one another's company. I was feeding my mind, however, and couldn't be troubled to make friends with janitors. But I was fascinated with Leon and would often watch the delight that he gained from the simple pleasure of his meal and the time spent with friends. I would often read Christian books (I recall reading Dietrich Bonhoeffer's *The Cost of Discipleship* at this time). Rather than developing friendships, I was feasting my pride. When I look back now, I see that my feeble attempts at self-education and Christian growth separated me from others. What should have been great opportunities for simple pleasures were perverted by my pride. I am now ashamed of my attitudes, my judgments, and my false pride.

I was unmasked (if only to myself) when Leon showed me his first driver's license. He was fifty when he received it. He had been driving and hauling trash illegally for years! Yet here he was pleased as punch to show his driver's license to me, the college boy. And then he asked me to read it to him. I suddenly realized why he had not obtained a driver's license prior to this time. Leon could not read. And yet he was so humble that he could ask me to read it to him. His sense of self was so strong, his lack of pride so evident, he could ask a college boy to read his license to him. And read it I did, every word a reproach to my failure at humility. If I hadn't been able to read, my pride surely would not have allowed me to ask someone to read my license. I was humiliated by his humility.

Leon had obtained by a hard life what I was hoping to attain through books — losing one's self. I realized that my fascination with Leon had been his ease with himself, his unpretentiousness, his ability to accept life as a gift, and now I saw that gleaming behind it all was humility. I had looked down on him for being "just a janitor," but now I felt

unworthy for my lack of humility. I may have been smarter, but morally
Leon was light-years ahead of me. He was one swift, kind kick in the
butt to my own moral development. I saw in him what I lacked. I had
much more to learn from him than he from me. Moment of grace.

angels unawares

When I lived on the east coast, I was often visited by a member of
our church at the most inconvenient times. Larry would show up on
Friday or Saturday evenings just before we were to meet friends for
pizza and a movie or early Saturday mornings when my deepest desire
was for more sleep. The exasperation I felt when this unwelcome
visitor would rouse me from sleep or interrupt my relaxation was
exacerbated by his unpleasant demeanor. Larry was extremely obese,
partially mentally retarded, and downright annoying in his demands
for attention. Members of the church would joke about the latest
victim of his inopportune visits. He often made the rounds until he
found someone who was willing to devote time to him. No one,
though, was eager for a surprise visit from Larry. He was doubly
annoying because he seemed unaware that we didn't want to be
bothered by him.

One Friday evening Larry stopped by and was especially dis-
traught. He had already tried to stop at the home of several other
members of the church but had been turned away. In tears Larry
described to me his loneliness, his bitterness at not being "normal,"
and his regularly rebuffed requests for companionship on weekends.
"Where else can I find friends, if not in a church?" he cried. At that
moment I saw Larry as a human being and not a smelly inconvenience.
He was created in the image of God. No longer did I see a worthless
mental defective; I was in the presence of an image-bearer of the
divine, a being of inestimable worth! The reflection of God shown
through those frail mounds of human flesh.

I recalled the verse: "Do not neglect to show hospitality to strangers, for thereby some have entertained angels unawares" (Heb. 13:2). I have wondered ever since if Larry was an unlikely angel. I might be wrong, but that moment of grace illuminated his true nature — if not as an angel, at least as an image-bearer of God. I knew then that Larry's demands could no longer be ignored, devalued, and laughed off. I could no longer neglect him. Moment of light?

moments of light

When my son Will was born, my wife and I were living in a tiny house. We were so excited about the birth of our first child, however, that we did not mind sharing our only bedroom with him. Our tiny roommate made sounds while he slept, sounds that to a non-parent might have seemed strange and disturbing, but to us they were music. We would often wake up and in our half-sleep anxiously listen for his baby-singing or at least his quiet breathing and then drift off to sleep, satisfied. Will did not sleep peacefully through every night, so we would swap turns walking with him in our living room. One evening the moonlight cascaded through a window and illuminated the face of my son. I was so grateful for Will that I lifted him up into the light and gave thanks to the Divine Father. I deeply felt Will was a *gift* — and gifts have givers. At that moment I believed that the Divine Father had given his child the gift of a son.

I now have three children — Will, Emily, and Evan — who are lights of my life. I can scarcely look at the three — playing with one another, laughing, sitting in my lap, caring for one another, taking a bath, or sleeping — without being immensely grateful. I have been gifted with three angels. (Make no mistake here, they are often fallen angels!) Moments of light.

the light of nature

I am most keenly aware of God when I leave the city and walk in the mountains. Cities are often dull, predictable, and tedious. Mile after mile of strip malls, ribbons of asphalt lined with ghastly, naked poles, unsightly architecture, people living too close to one another — these are hardly tributes to the human spirit. It is only when the layers of human development are peeled away that I feel in touch with the divine. Under the immense starry sky or within vast arboreal canyons, while clinging to the side of a majestic mountain or lightly sleeping amidst bears and moose, I am reminded of my finitude and that the world is a creation. And if there is a creation, there is a Creator. Cities manifest the human; mountains reveal the divine.

> The heavens declare the glory of God;
>> the skies proclaim the work of his hands.
> Day after day they pour forth speech;
>> night after night they display knowledge.
>
> Psalm 19:1-2, NIV

Wordsworth, too, saw God in nature. In his poem *Tintern Abbey* he describes how the wild ecstasies of unreflective youth have been superseded by the insights of maturity. The mountains, rivers, and valleys, once merely a playground for the exercise of gleeful and innocent passions, have become the arena for perceiving the divine anchor and guardian of his soul. The loss of his childhood joy has been replaced by a greater gift — the mature experience, now tinged with the sadness of knowing human suffering, that enlivens the heart and mind to read the deeper meaning of the rolling brook and the majestic mountains. If one is quiet one may hear the still small voice of God. Wordsworth recounts the soothing value of returning to the woods when he feels world weary. Now in the woods, he finds that his hope and faith are revived:

Therefore am I still
A lover of the meadows and the woods,
And mountains; and all that we behold
.... I am well pleased to recognise
In nature and the language of the sense,
The anchor of my purest thoughts, the nurse,
The guide, the guardian of my heart, and soul
Of all my moral being.

Wordsworth, *Lines Written a
Few Miles above Tintern Abbey*

Mountains remind us of divine majesty; rivers and oceans, of awesome power and passing time; prairies, of limitless space and empty silence; trees and flowers, of providential goodness and beauty; peculiar animals, of God's wistful creativity; stars, of terrifying immensity and our puny finitude. Kathleen Norris writes of the wisdom that may be discerned from the vast plains of the Dakotas:

A person is forced inward by the spareness of what is outward and visible in all this land and sky. The beauty of the Plains is like that of an icon; it does not give an inch to sentimentality or romance. The flow of the land, with its odd twists and buttes, is like the flow of Gregorian chant that rises and falls beyond melody, beyond reason or human expectation, but perfectly. Maybe seeing the Plains is like seeing an icon: what seems stern and almost empty is merely open, a door into some simple and holy state.[1]

By gleaning the field of nature we can learn both that we are truly insignificant and that God created all of this wonderful stuff for us.

1. Kathleen Norris, *Dakota: A Spiritual Geography* (New York: Ticknor and Fields, 1993), 157.

seeing God in nature

Seeing God in nature demands that we see as a child. As we grow older, we get more deeply encased in a protective shell — of house, automobile, office, mall, and self — that cuts us off from reality. We watch nature on television, but we rarely see it directly. The incessant yet innocent "Why" of children has been drummed out of them by tranquilized adults who have lost their sense of wonder. As we grow up, we cease asking questions of nature (whose answers would seize us with delight). We cozy up to the familiar and refuse to bump against mystery and grandeur. We think we are masters of the universe when actually we will soon be conquered by it. We are comfortable, our climate under control, but insensible; we are once, twice, or thrice removed from nature. And the farther we remove ourselves from creation, the farther we remove ourselves from our Creator.

Annie Dillard manifests the mystery of God in nature. In *Pilgrim at Tinker Creek* she encourages stalking and exploring both nature and God. And she who seeks, finds — in this case, the hidden wonders of God's grace in the world. But God is hidden, and seeing God in nature requires having a gift of spiritual illumination. Although Dillard doesn't create the light, she does manage to get in its way, to notice it. And like Moses on Mt. Sinai, she has been graced with a vision of the back parts of God:

> And then occasionally the mountains part. The tree with the lights in it appears, the mockingbird falls, and time unfurls across space like an oriflamme. Now we rejoice. . . . I wait on the bridges and stalk along the banks for those moments I cannot predict, when a wave begins to surge under the water, and ripples strengthen and pulse high across the creek and back again in a texture that throbs. It is like the surfacing of an impulse, like the materialization of a fish, this rising, this coming to a head, like the ripening nutmeats still in their husks, ready to split open like buckeyes in a field, shining

with newness. "Surely the Lord is in this place; and I knew it not." The fleeing shreds I see, the back parts, are a gift, an abundance. When Moses came down from the cleft in Mount Sinai, the people were afraid of him: the very skin on his face shone.[2]

And then all we can do in the face of this spectacular light show is gratefully stand in awe and take off our shoes because, like Moses, we are standing on holy ground.

facts as miracles

When I reflect upon my life, I occasionally view it as a totality of events through which God has graciously shaped me. I sometimes see my ups and downs, my meager victories and major defeats, my righteousness and my self-righteousness, my family and friends and my choices as a meaningful pattern that God is weaving together. G. K. Chesterton writes: "I had always vaguely felt facts to be miracles. . . ."[3] My life is not simply a meaningless conglomeration of serendipitous events and unremarkable happenstance. Rather, it is a series of divine appointments with the goal of shaping my character. God may be experienced not only in specific moments of light but also when reflecting on the course of a life.

Have the significant events of my life been determined by the random movement of atoms, by arbitrary and essentially meaningless free choices, or by a benevolent providence working through my shortcomings? I look at my life now and think of the remarkable confluence of events, people, and choices that have shaped and equipped me for my present tasks and relationships. I have been

2. Annie Dillard, *Pilgrim at Tinker Creek* (New York: Harper's Magazine Press, 1974), 205.

3. Gilbert Keith Chesterton, *Orthodoxy* (New York: John Lane, 1909), 109.

rescued from divorce, a career in church ministry (for which I am temperamentally unsuited), intolerant dogmatism, suffering, and a host of wrong choices. I would not choose to repeat some of my formative and painful past, but it has shaped me in ways I could not have foreseen. Was all this serendipitous happenstance or was it divine providence? If I have been rescued, who or what is my Rescuer?

In 1980 I worked for a church in Des Moines, Iowa. One late wintry evening I slowly pulled out of the church parking lot, eager for the break of night. I turned on the radio and heard that the occasional flurries were about to settle into a vicious winter storm. Perhaps the roads would be impassable tomorrow, I thought, and I could sleep in and spend the day relaxing with my wife.

As I pulled the car onto the interstate, I noticed through the snowy haze a person sitting on the side of the road with his thumb extended. Exhausted and eager to get home, I hoped against hope that he would not catch my eye, that I would not feel guilty ignoring a human being about to be swallowed by a midwestern gale. But I could not ignore him. I pulled my car over and invited him in.

He entered my car reeking of alcohol, and his erratic behavior made me wonder if that was the only foreign substance infecting his body. I found out that he was headed to Omaha, but it was unlikely that he would be able to hitchhike there on this blustery night. Since he had no money, I invited him to spend the night at our house. As we drove along, he began to tell me about his wretched life and about how he was hoping to start anew in Omaha. He confessed an addiction to alcohol and drugs that he desperately wished to overcome.

As we entered our house, I explained the appearance of this mysterious and unbecoming stranger to my wife. She was understandably alarmed that her husband had brought home a strung out, penniless stranger, but she agreed to let him sleep on our couch. I prepared his bed, and my wife and I went off to ours.

We heard a great deal of rattling around downstairs and began to fear what might be happening. I closed our door and pushed a dresser in front of it for safety. A short time later, we heard the door to our patio open, and I rushed to the window thinking that I would watch him sneak off, perhaps with our checkbook or other valuables. As I peered down, I noticed that he was relieving himself off the side of our deck! When he came back inside, my wife insisted that I go down and take him to a hotel.

I went down determined to do my husbandly duty. But when I walked into the intruder's room, I saw him sitting on the couch reading our Bible. Tears were streaming down his face as he began to tell me about his awful life and to ask me about God. Rather than take him to the hotel, I stayed up several more hours talking with him.

When we awoke the next morning, I called the only pastor in my denomination in Omaha and asked if he could meet this fellow in Omaha. Coincidentally or providentially, the pastor told me that his church directed a live-in drug and alcohol rehabilitation center and that he would have a counselor meet my new friend at the bus station. Were the facts of this young man's life evincing a miracle? Again: serendipitous happenstance or divine providence?

the light of reason

Some Christian apologists have attempted to meet doubt with proof. G. K. Chesterton, for example, felt that the universe does not explain itself but must have a purpose — life is a story with a plot; there must be a story-teller. Stripped of his elegant prose, his thought is that the best explanation of the existence, order, and purpose of the universe is an Orderer and Designer. This god of order and purpose deserves our worship.

What are our options for explaining the existence and order of the universe? Chesterton thinks that naturalistic explanations are wanting, and he therefore embraces a supernatural explanation. This magical, beautiful universe has some meaning or purpose, Chesterton

31

contends, and the appropriate response to the Magician is thanksgiving and humility. This is Chesterton's case for rational belief in God.

After making his case for theism, Chesterton chastises contemporary doubters for their intellectual impotence and excessive skepticism. He writes: "But what we suffer from to-day is humility in the wrong place. Modesty has moved from the organ of ambition. Modesty has settled upon the organ of conviction; where it was never meant to be."[4] Although quite clever, Chesterton seems quite wrong; in this age of uncertainty, humility may be precisely what is (and what has always been) required concerning our beliefs. It is ironic that Chesterton's own case for Christianity is built on "stubborn and subtle emotions" and on a succession of qualifiers like "perhaps," "it seems," and "maybe."

While belief in God may provide the intellectual and moral center of our lives, we may still not be certain of its truth. We have been endowed with cognitive faculties that generally allow us to acquire true beliefs. God has also given us the ability to test and question our beliefs. This ability is a blessing and a curse; every significant and fundamental belief is inevitably attended with a thousand questions. Would that our reasoning capabilities were infallible, but they are not. Theist and atheist alike must attempt a comprehensive understanding of the world on the basis of fallible, and often feeble, reasoning. The illumination of reason is insufficient to compel universal and facile consent on most matters of fundamental human concern. Not all atheists are fools or idiots. Intellectual humility is a virtue that recognizes the limits of human understanding. The corresponding vice is an uncritical dogmatism that is intolerant of alternative beliefs and immune to criticism. We ought to have our settled convictions, but we should be aware of their limitations and remain open to legitimate criticism of them.

4. Chesterton, *Orthodoxy*, 55.

the verdict

Can a reasonable case be made in favor of belief in God? Or is belief in God arbitrary or irrational? Let me suggest how such a case might be developed.

Suppose that you are on a jury and that God is on trial. God is the defendant. Suppose that no one has seen or heard the defendant in millennia and longer. Suppose further that the job of the defense attorney is to prove that the defendant exists and that the prosecuting attorney's task is to prove that he does not exist. The jury is initially divided. Some are wholeheartedly committed to his existence, some only halfheartedly so; some are simply agnostic, and some are dead set against his existence.

The prosecuting attorney makes his case. No one has seen God. If he exists, he has failed to show up for this trial. Surely it would be little trouble for God to make an appearance if he did exist. And surely he would want people to be aware of his existence so that they could learn to relate to him appropriately. His absence is remarkable. As we examine the evidence to see if he has been here, perhaps unrecognized, we find a world wallowing in pain and misery. The evidence proves that God does not exist.

The defense attorney presents the following evidence. Although she has no pictures of God, she can show traces, as it were, of God's fingerprints and footprints. God has left divine marks on the universe that are evident to attentive minds. So the defense attorney asks the jury to consider the following: We see around us a universe of remarkable order that allows for the existence of human beings who have a deep moral sense, who can make significant moral choices, and who are capable of responding to a divine being (if there is one). There have been reports of miracles, alleged religious experiences, and near-death experiences of this divine being.

To demonstrate the remarkable design of the universe, the defense attorney calls a host of Nobel-prize–winning physicists. They

33

testify to the astounding confluence of physical constants that are necessary to create and sustain human life. The big bang and the subsequent development of the cosmos depend upon a number of these constants. The universe is amazingly fine-tuned for the existence of human life. The physicists present the following testimony:

1. *The rate of expansion:* if the rate of the universe's expansion were slightly stronger ($1/10^{55}$ stronger), the infant universe would have collapsed too soon to allow for galaxies to form. If the rate of expansion were slightly weaker, the cosmos would have expanded too rapidly to allow for the formation of galaxies. The rate of expansion is precisely attuned to the existence of human life.

2. *The electromagnetic force:* if the electromagnetic force (a fundamental physical force responsible for the interactions between charged particles) were slightly stronger, stars would be too cold to allow life to form on their planets. If it were slightly weaker, every star would be too hot and short-lived to sustain life. Electromagnetism is precisely attuned to the existence of human life.

3. *The weak nuclear force:* if the weak nuclear force (a fundamental physical force governing the interactions of subatomic particles) were appreciably stronger, the big bang would have converted all of the hydrogen in the universe into helium. This would mean no water. And if no water, no life as we know it. The weak nuclear force is precisely attuned to the existence of life.

As the procession of witnesses continues, the number and precision of the physical constants necessary for physical life become more apparent. Even the prosecuting attorney accepts these claims as fact. A dazzling case has been made that the universe seems particularly fine-tuned for human life. "Is it by design or by accident that this is so?" the defense attorney asks.

She asks the jury to consider the following example. She takes a deck of cards, shuffles them ten times, and then deals them. When she deals the cards, they come out in the following order: the ace of spades through the king of spades, then the ace of hearts through the king of hearts, then the ace of clubs through the king of clubs, and then the ace of diamonds through the king of diamonds. What would you think? What are the options for explaining the remarkable order of the cards? Either the cards were stacked by the dealer, or their order is simply a coincidence. Random coincidence is a possibility, but it would be unreasonable to believe that the cards attained their astounding order by such a process. The only reasonable explanation is that an intelligent and skilled dealer stacked the deck in favor of this order.

So much for the cards. What about the universe as we know it? That the physical constants necessary for the existence and life-supporting capacity of the universe come about by chance is infinitely more unlikely than that the cards in the illustration owe their order to chance. It is highly improbable that *only by chance* are all of the relevant physical constants precisely the way they are, that *only by chance* is the combination of these constants precisely what it is, and that *only by chance* do the constants and their combination allow for the existence of human life. The only reasonable explanation for the existence of human life is that the universe has a supremely intelligent and maximally skilled designer.[5]

So the defense attorney takes us back to her original evidence: the existence of an ordered universe that permits the existence of human beings with a moral sense and with intimations of a divine being. Is the evidence better explained by chance or by an omniscient, omnipotent, wholly good creator who desires creatures capable of entering freely into relationship with him? Given that it is possible but infinitely improbable to explain the evidence as a mere random process, it is more reasonable to believe that God created the universe. Reason and experience lead one to embrace the existence of God. Case closed.

5. See John Leslie, *Universes* (New York: Routledge, 1989).

chapter 3

Moments
of Darkness

This is what I see and what troubles me. I look on all sides, and I see only darkness everywhere. Nature presents to me nothing which is not a matter of doubt and concern. If I saw nothing there which revealed a Divinity, I would come to a negative conclusion; if I saw everywhere the signs of a Creator, I would remain peacefully in faith. But, seeing too much to deny and too little to be sure, I am in a state to be pitied.

Blaise Pascal, *Pensées*

Meanwhile, where is God? This is one of the most disquieting symptoms. When you are happy, so happy that you have no sense of needing Him, so happy that you are tempted to feel His claims upon you as an interruption, if you remember yourself and turn to Him with gratitude and praise, you will be — or so it feels — welcomed with open arms. But go to Him when your need is desperate, when all other help is vain, and what do you find? A door slammed in your face, and a sound of bolting and double bolting on the inside. After that, silence. You may as well turn away. The longer you wait, the more emphatic the silence will become. There are no lights in the windows. It might be an empty house. Was it ever inhabited? It seemed so once. And that seeming was as strong as this. What can this mean? Why is He so present a commander in our time of prosperity and so very absent a help in time of trouble?

C. S. Lewis, *A Grief Observed*

ooooo

In the preceding chapter the lights of reason and experience coalesced into a grounding for belief in God. The case is closed. Or is it? We live in darkness, but there is sufficient light to guide our moral and spiritual journey. We see through the glass darkly, but at least we can see through the glass. Pascal, however, reminds us of our contradictory nature — that we are both believing and unbelieving, desiring certainty but remaining unsure of our deepest commitment. Unlike the animals, who care little for their future and are unconcerned for their souls, we humans are conscious and self-conscious. We are aware of our needs and desires but are unconvinced that they will ultimately be satisfied. Our consciousness and self-consciousness extend well beyond the needs of mere survival. We see "too much to deny and too little to be sure." We are the most pitiable of all creatures. We have visions of light, yet we are plunged into darkness.

illumination or illusion?

There are times when I wonder if my moments of light are illumination or illusion. Are they patterns of grace or remarkable coincidence? I sometimes lie awake at night and question my deepest beliefs. I find it hard to get a fix on them, and I worry that they all might not be true. How can I believe in divine providence when there has been more human slaughter in our century than in any previous century? Does God not exist, or does he simply not care? Why is he hidden in our times of deepest need? How can it be that God became a man so long ago and that he expects everyone to believe that this Jesus bore our sins and rose again from the dead? It seems so unlikely. Don't we all know that dead men stay dead? Is my life really a miracle? Is it all true?

When I am reading C. S. Lewis, God's existence and goodness seem not only likely but inevitable. I feel confident in my belief; my doubts beat a hasty retreat. But then I walk away and the doubts return. Lewis makes heaven seem just as vivid as a land called Narnia with talking animals. For a brief time, I can enter imaginatively into the world of Narnia but I quickly reenter the world of reality. I have a similar experience with his serious religious writings — am I only believing what I wish to be true when I read Lewis on Narnia and heaven? My moments of light dim into moments of darkness.

I realize, of course, that I may have been deceived by all my moments of light — that all my glimpses of the divine are just illusion. Part of the terror of life in this age of uncertainty is the realization that all of my most fundamental beliefs might be utterly wrong. My entire life might be structured around a lie. But these apparent manifestations of the divine ground my trust in God. My best understanding of the pattern of my life is that these moments of light are divine gifts and serve to direct me towards God. But perhaps my best understanding is simply self-deception.

providence or pain?

When I moved to the Midwest, I lost touch with Larry. I spoke with him recently over the telephone and learned that he had been in a terrible automobile accident that cost him the use of his arms and caused him excruciating pain for well over a year. His normal loneliness increased exponentially; he was seldom visited either in the hospital or at his home during his convalescence. He recounted the agony of the physical pain and the emotional anguish of feeling abandoned by his friends. I was struck at that point with how unfair it all seemed. Why did Larry have to suffer so? He was as low as anyone I knew and did not seem to need more pain and isolation to bring him closer to God. I could not see any salutary effect that further suffering could have on him. Suffering could only further degrade him, not make him more human. I could not see a wonderful, divine pattern in Larry's life, only chaos and degradation. Moment of darkness.

Although God seemed to have taught me a lesson through Larry about judging on appearances, undervaluing one of his creatures and the prominence of pride in my life, what lessons could he be teaching Larry? Was Larry's life directed by providence or by pain? What advantage could suffering gain for him?

torture and God

During a trip to Europe, I visited a museum in Belgium. On display were gruesome instruments of torture designed to maximize suffering. The famed Iron Maiden was there — with her cold metal cocoon encasing a hundred sharpened spines, which when closed would pierce the body of her victims. The spines were carefully arranged to avoid hitting vital organs, thus keeping the sufferer alive interminably. The instruments of pain were accompanied by instructions from a seventeenth-century manual of torture as well as engravings that depicted actual events. I was struck by two of the devices. The first was a vise-like instrument that squeezed a person's chin and the top of his head. The dispenser of the punishment was carefully instructed to tighten the vise very slowly, thereby inflicting the most pain possible, all the while keeping the victim conscious. As the vise slowly and painfully closed, the manual continued, the teeth would first break and then powder, next the jaw would crack, then the skull would split, the brains would begin to ooze out, and finally the victim would lose consciousness and die after hours of suffering.

The most gruesome depiction of torture I encountered did not require the sophisticated technology of the vise or the Iron Maiden. The only requirements here were a cart and two logs. The victim's arm was positioned carefully on top of the logs, leaving enough room for a heavy wagon wheel to be driven over it, thereby breaking the bone; next, the other arm was broken, and then the legs, and then the hands. Eventually, every bone in the body was broken. The back was broken last, in several places, and then the victim was strapped at the

41

waist to the center of a wheel placed vertically on an axle. The person was spun mercilessly around and around. Eventually, after an unimaginably long period of conscious, excruciating pain, he would die.

The very invention of such instruments of torture is as shocking as their actual use. Why were these tortures designed to delay death and prolong pain and suffering interminably? After all, death could be accomplished in an instant by slicing off the head. In the seventeenth century the answer was clear — to allow enough time for the victim to reconsider the error of his ways, to recant heretical religious beliefs, and to confess the one true religion. For the Inquisition, the way to fidelity was torture. Suffering inflicted in the name of God.

nature red in tooth and claw

In a wonderful PBS television special on lions, I was struck by the maternal care of a lioness for her cubs. Wonderful filming caught the birth, feeding, and tender play of the cubs within the peaceful, pastoral setting of the African plains. This gentle vision was shattered by the stark realities of life and death. The lions hunted and killed a gazelle and set to feast on the warm carcass. In a shocking scene at the feeding, the lioness gazed into the camera, her muzzle dripping fresh blood. Most terrifying was the sight of the mother attacking her own cubs as they tried to feed. Mixed with the blood of the gazelle was the blood of her own offspring. Nature is, as Darwin was fond of saying, "red in tooth and claw." Annie Dillard recounts a more gruesome variation on the same theme: "Even such sophisticated mammals as the great predator cats occasionally eat their cubs. A mother cat will be observed licking the area around the umbilical cord of the helpless newborn. She licks, she licks, she licks until something snaps in her brain, and she begins eating, starting there, at the vulnerable belly."[1]

1. Annie Dillard, *Pilgrim at Tinker Creek* (New York: Harper's Magazine Press, 1974), 169.

42

I once saw a film showing a female wasp breaking into the earthen home of a caterpillar. The wasp injected an egg deep inside the soft belly of the caterpillar and then turned and went off forever. The egg grew slowly, gradually devouring its reluctant host from the inside. At the end of its gestation period, the caterpillar undulated spasmodically and erupted into a fully grown wasp. The parasitic wasp had eaten its juicy host from the inside and emerged by shedding its protective tent. If the female wasp were unable to find a caterpillar in which to lay her eggs, the young would simply eat their mother from the inside.

Animals tear other animals to shreds and then devour them, their prey sometimes still alive to be eaten away by digestive juices. Mothers eat their infants. Infants feed on their parents. Some birds give birth to two offspring, and the larger offspring push the smaller out of the nest. This is no fluke — it is written into this species' design and repeated endlessly.

The world of nature includes vastly more death than life. Of all the species that have ever existed, fewer than five percent are still alive. Whole species have proven incapable of surviving on a planet created precisely for them. Of every creature born, few survive infancy. Eggs and babies make most excellent meals. Each cupful of ocean water is littered with countless dead parasites, barnacle larvae, and plankton. Dillard comments: "I have to acknowledge that the sea is a cup of death and the land is a stained altar stone. We the living are survivors huddled on flotsam, living on jetsam. We are escapees. We wake in terror, eat in hunger, sleep with a mouthful of blood."[2]

In the midst of this awful waste, does the cosmos care more for us than it does for barnacle larvae? Are we magnificent yet superfluous permutations of matter? Are we simply part of the wasteful stupidity that governs the rest of life? Are we to believe that there is a creator who cares not for the infants of lions, the bellies of caterpillars, or the smallest of birds but who does care for us? Who do we think we are?

2. Dillard, *Pilgrim at Tinker Creek*, 175.

The world seems uniquely designed for our demise as well. We don't seem special. In some countries, fewer than fifty percent of babies survive infancy. Of those who do, many are malnourished, physically or mentally deformed, and in no position to improve their lot in life. With Western medicine, humans have conspired to do what God has never bothered to do — protect and prolong the life of innocents. Why won't God lift a finger, at least for the little ones?

the suffering of innocents

In *The Brothers Karamazov* Dostoevski has Ivan Karamazov raise the problem of innocent suffering. One can only recoil at the suggestion that the child in the following example deserved her suffering:

> There's [a story] about a little five-year-old girl, hated by her parents, who are described as "most respectable and socially prominent people, cultured and well-educated." . . . And so these refined parents subjected their five-year-old girl to all kinds of torture. They beat her, kicked her, flogged her, for no reason that they themselves knew of. The child's whole body was covered with bruises. Eventually they devised a new refinement . . . they forced her to eat excrement, smearing it all over her face. And it was the mother who did it! And then that woman would lock her little daughter up in the outhouse until morning and she did so even on the coldest nights, when it was freezing. Imagine the little creature, unable even to understand what is happening to her, beating her sore little chest with her tiny fist, weeping hot, unresentful tears, and begging "gentle Jesus" to help her, and all this happening in that icy, dark, stinking place!"[3]

3. Fyodor Dostoevski, *The Brothers Karamazov*, trans. Richard Pevear and Larissa Volokhonsky (San Francisco: North Point Publishing, 1990), 242.

Ivan, in a conversation with his brother Alyosha, makes a case for atheism based on the innocent suffering of children. Alyosha is a monk, cloistered within the confines of a protective environment. In a classic confrontation between simple believer and worldly unbeliever, Dostoevsky discusses the problem that human suffering raises for Christian belief. Ivan contends that the Christian is expected to believe that parallel lines, which never meet on earth, will meet in infinity.

This powerful image captures the difficulty of reconciling belief in God with the suffering of the innocent, especially children. The Christian sees no redemption for the suffering of innocents in this life, but is called to believe that they will be redeemed in the next life. As Ivan puts it, the Christian must believe that

> Suffering will be healed and made up for . . . at the moment of eternal harmony, something so precious will come to pass that it will suffice for all hearts, for the comforting of all resentments, for the atonement of all crimes of humanity, of all the blood they've shed; that it will make it not only possible to forgive, but to justify all that has happened with men.[4]

Although he is able to express this hope better than most Christians, it is precisely this hope for eternal harmony that Ivan is unable to accept. He cannot believe that the parallel lines will meet in heaven. Why? Because heaven exacts too high a price with the suffering of children.

The Psalmists regularly lament not only the suffering of the righteous but also the prospering of the wicked. The scales of justice, which apportion rewards to goodness and punishment to wickedness, are clearly unbalanced in our short lifetime. As McDuff, on hearing of the slaughter of his wife and children, cries: "Did heaven look on, And would not take their part?" (*Macbeth*, 5.1.225-26).

4. Dostoevski, *The Brothers Karamazov*, 235.

For a short time we lived near a "bad" neighborhood with a house that distributed crack cocaine. I walked by one day and saw two small boys playing on the front lawn outside the crack house. I was mesmerized by their play; it was the play of innocent children — undistracted and unpretentious. I was caught up in their smiles and youthful laughter. They seemed like angels in their rapturous simplicity and delight. This peaceful scene was shattered by the entrance of an adult (perhaps an addict) who began to scream obscenities at her children. I was moved by a sense of injustice and sadness. Injustice, because a child growing up in this kind of neighborhood with an addict for a parent and subject to that kind of abuse did not have a fair chance at a normal, happy life. Sadness, because of how fast these children had to give up their innocence. They were being robbed of their present childhood and their future happiness. Why should one's potential for peace, happiness, prosperity, education, and well-being depend so much on the accidents of birth? Why are the iniquities of the fathers (and mothers) visited upon the children unto the third and fourth generation? Why the children?

two musics unto men

Arthur Clough, a nineteenth-century British poet, was consumed with both belief and doubt. Deep within his anguished doubts, there is always a longing to believe, a persistent hope that the Christian story is true. Though wanting to believe firmly, he wavered: "So constant as my heart would be, / So fickle as it must. . . ." So he always listened for the voice of God. But how quickly that still small voice of God becomes fainter and fainter as it recedes into the recesses of our dim memory. God's quiescence diminishes to a deafening silence. In the following poetic description of the divided self, Clough writes of straining to hear God's quiet voice amidst the overpowering din of his ordinary life:

46

Are there not, then, two musics unto men? —
One loud and bold and coarse,
And overpowering still perforce
All tone and tune beside;
Yet in despite its pride
Only of fumes of foolish fancy bred,
And sounding solely in the sounding head:
The other, soft and low,
Stealing whence we not know,
Painfully heard and easily forgot,
With pauses oft and many a silence strange,
(And silent oft it seems, when silent it is not)
Revivals too of unexpected change:
Haply thou think'st 'twill never be begun,
Or that't has come, and been, and passed away;
Yet turn to other none, —
Turn not, oh, turn not thou!
But listen, listen, listen, — if haply be heard it may;
Listen, listen, listen, — is it not sounding now?[5]

Arthur Clough, *Qui Laborat, Orat*

my grief observed

In 1987 my father suddenly died a few days before Thanksgiving. I had not seen him since the preceding Christmas and was eagerly anticipating the holiday visit. Two days before we were to arrive, my brother called and delivered the news. Rather than celebrate Thanksgiving, we mourned my father's death. My initial reaction was denial:

5. H. F. Lowry, A. L. P. Norrington, F. L. Mulhauser, eds., *The Poems of A. H. Clough* (Oxford: Clarendon Press, 1951), 22-23.

when I returned home, he would be sitting in his usual chair, wearing his favorite flannel shirt, watching the Detroit Lions; we would go out for a walk in his garden to get the lone cauliflower that had survived fall's frost. At the viewing, I looked on his body lying in a fancy lacquered box, "resting peacefully," as the expression goes, as if he were asleep and soon to rise. Drawing closer, I saw his ashen face, touched his hardened body, and felt the lack of the living's warmth. Denial no longer possible, I felt the sharp pain of my dad's death.

I was gripped by the loss of my father. Rather than rejoicing that he was "in a better place now," that "he died doing what he wanted," that "he had lived a full life," I was convinced that death had finally won and that the eternal separation of father and son had begun. Never before had I experienced such a profound sense of unbelief. The apostle Paul was wrong—death did have its victory and its sting. I mourned as one who had no hope. My father was simply his body, and there it lay—stiff and lifeless, forever.

A week or two after my father's death, I watched the television film *Shadowlands,* the story of C. S. Lewis's marriage to Joy Davidman. Joy converted to Christianity in part because of the influence of Lewis's writings. After a lengthy correspondence, Joy, an American, came to England and they became fast friends. Shortly thereafter, Joy contracted cancer. The movie suggests that Lewis secretly married Joy so that she could stay in England and receive British medical care for her debilitating affliction. Although Joy battled valiantly and Lewis came to love her dearly, she eventually lost her struggle. Joy's death plunged Lewis into a long and deep depression as well as a crisis of faith. The movie depicts many conversations between Lewis and his rector. The rector grows exasperated with Lewis and asks what he is so afraid of. Lewis, in a profound statement of unbelief, replies: "I fear I may never see her again." In *A Grief Observed,* his journal of dealing with Joy's death, Lewis writes:

After the death of a friend, years ago, I had for some time a most vivid feeling of certainty about his continued life; even his enhanced life. I have begged to be given even one hundredth part of the same assurance about H. [Joy]. There is no answer. Only the locked door, the iron curtain, the vacuum, absolute zero. "Them as asks don't get." I was a fool to ask.[6]

Lewis came to see that life-and-death situations reveal how much we really believe.

My contradictory beliefs, the two musics to which I was listening, were revealed (if only to me) only days after my father's death when I was asked to deliver the eulogy at his funeral. I had recently been plunged into the depths of unbelief, but now I was called upon to express my faith. So I spoke of my father's character — his kindness, compassion, patience, commitment to justice, and devotion to his family. I concluded by expressing my feeble hope in the resurrection.

We vastly overestimate our faith (as we do our goodness and wisdom). Propped up by our feeble rituals, our pat answers, our multitude of activities designed (perhaps subconsciously) to prevent us from seeing our true and divided self, we believe that we are men and women of God, ready to perish by Caesar's sword. In *A Grief Observed*, Lewis, regarded by so many as a giant of the faith, confesses:

> God has not been trying an experiment on my faith or love in order to find out their quality. He knew it already. It was I who didn't. In this trial He makes us occupy the dock, the witness box, and the bench all at once. He always knew that my temple was a house of cards. His only way of making me realize the fact was to knock it down.[7]

6. C. S. Lewis, *A Grief Observed* (New York: Bantam, 1976), 7.
7. Lewis, *A Grief Observed*, 61.

Why do I feel better knowing that Lewis, the most famous apologist of the twentieth century, doubted the existence of heaven and the goodness of God? Is it just that the misery of doubt loves company?

inviting and dangerous

I once hiked with a group into a magnificent ice cave in Idaho. We entered through a small opening in the side of the mountain and found ourselves in a natural wonderland. Outside it was 85° but inside it was freezing. The floor was covered with a solid sheet of thick ice. The walls sparkled like diamonds as the light from our headlamps bounced off of them. The passageway narrowed and dropped and rose and widened, with an eerie flow of air that maintained its frigid temperatures passing our chilly ears. The risings and fallings of the floor called for care. Our headlamps pointed only where we looked, and by staring straight ahead we risked overlooking a steep drop in the floor. A single misstep on an icy ramp could have meant a long, uncontrollable slide to certain injury. So we looked in all directions. Our battery-driven lights looked like so many tiny searchlights as we tried to keep from banging our heads on the walls and ceiling and from falling in a disastrous tumble.

At the end of the walkway was a huge cavern of ice. On the floor was a smooth frozen lake, and at the far end was a giant icicle. The icicle was close to twenty feet in diameter, and it extended above and below where the eye could see. The grandeur of the cave and our corresponding tininess combined to make us feel giddy with delight. The appeal of the room was nearly irresistible—to skate across the frozen lake and lick the immense icicle! But our guide tempered our unbridled enthusiasm with wisdom; he pointed out that the frozen lake was at an angle and that the icicle was suspended in a large vertical shaft that dropped down hundreds of feet. One slip on the icy pond and there would be no stopping until the bottom of the vertical tunnel. Many people had been lured by the magic of this cave to their deaths. Our dim and narrow lamps had deceived us — what appeared to us as beautiful and inviting was a deadly snare.

The leap of our faith is equally compelling and dangerous. We are asked to sell all to gain the pearl of great price. Faith in God costs everything: our time and possessions, our relationships and commitments, our secret selves, our very lives. But what God takes away with his left hand he gives back again with his right. We gain peace, patience, kindness, goodness, rest for our souls, and bliss eternal. The lure is enticing — eternal life and unending relationships with others and God. But our lamps are dim and narrow. On our next step we may tumble to death without resurrection. We look around in all directions, but we can't see clearly if the Jesus who appears to us is the Christ.

chapter 4

Fear and
Trembling

After these things God tested Abraham. He said to him, "Abraham!" And he said, "Here I am." He said, "Take your son, your only son Isaac, whom you love, and go to the land of Moriah, and offer him there as a burnt offering on one of the mountains that I shall show you."

Genesis 22:1-2

Faith is a terribly caustic substance, a burning acid. It puts to the test every element of my life and society; it spares nothing. It leads me ineluctably to question all my certitudes, all my moralities, beliefs, and policies. It forbids me to attach ultimate significance to any expression of human activity. It detaches and delivers me from money and the family, from my job and my knowledge. . . . Faith leaves nothing intact. . . . If my faith isn't the very same kind that Abraham had, it's nothing. It's as simple as that. Faith inevitably leads me to this measuring up, this fateful encounter — either Abraham's sort of faith or nothing. And so the only thing that faith can bring me to recognize is my impotence, my incapacity, my inadequacy, my incompleteness, and consequently my incredulity (naturally faith is the most unerring and lethal weapon against all beliefs). But that's precisely what makes it faith; that's how it exists and how it shapes me.

Jacques Ellul, *Living Faith: Belief and Doubt in a Perilous World*

ooooo

The world is a source of both illumination and obscurity, and this is cause for our deepest despair. We feel led to an impasse in our beliefs. We feel called to commitment, but our minds constrain our hearts and prevent us from fully heeding that call. What are we to do? In this chapter we will discuss the nature of faith as expressed in Scripture, focusing especially on the story of Abraham, the "father of our faith." Our guide here will be the Danish philosopher Søren Kierkegaard. His writings have aroused Christians from benignly slumbering in their beliefs and called them to commit themselves passionately to Christ. Kierkegaard awakens us to the demands of faith.

the roll call of faith

The roll call of faith in Hebrews 11 lauds our spiritual ancestors Abel, Noah, Abraham, Isaac, Jacob, Joseph, Moses, Rahab, Gideon, Barak, Samson, Jephthah, David, Samuel, and the prophets, who by faith "conquered kingdoms, administered justice, and obtained promises." No doubt these people are especially praiseworthy for their faithful actions in service to Yahweh. But the Scriptures are also painfully honest about their lack of commitment and their disobedience. Noah got drunk and lay naked for his youngest son to see. Abraham and Isaac both lied to protect themselves (Abraham twice) and tried to pass off their wives as their sisters. Jacob deceived his father to gain his brother's birthright. Moses failed to follow God's orders and therefore never entered the promised land. Rahab was a harlot. David, supposedly a man after God's own heart, was a murderer and an adulterer.

Gideon's inclusion in this list is most curious. Both an angel and the Lord himself appeared to Gideon to declare that he would be the mighty warrior to free the Israelites from the oppression of the Midianites (Judges 6). But his clan was the weakest, and he was the least of his clan, so he questioned God's choice of a savior. God gave Gideon a sign — fire miraculously flared from a rock and consumed a portion of bread and meat. Now convinced that the message was from God, Gideon built an altar to the Lord. As the Midianites and their allies gathered strength and amassed at their borders to attack Israel, Gideon, full of the spirit of the Lord, asked God to give him one more sign that he would be the savior of Israel. He placed a wool fleece on the threshing floor and asked the Lord to cover it with dew while leaving the ground around it dry. The Lord complied. But one fleece was not enough to convince Gideon, so he "fleeced" the Lord a second time. Again the Lord complied. Then Gideon went out and defeated his enemies. Gideon sounded the trumpet of the Lord. In the end, however, Gideon the hero turned to idolatry. "Gideon made an ephod of it [gold] and put it in his town, in Ophrah; and all Israel prostituted themselves to it there, and it became a snare to Gideon and to his family" (Judg. 8:27). Gideon's story ends in an ugly smear. It takes the call of an angel and of the Lord himself, a miracle, and two fleecings to convince Gideon, hero of the faith, of God's promise. How can we be expected not to doubt when our fleeces return dry so many times?

the faith of Abraham

Let us turn to Abraham, "the father of our faith." Abraham believed God when God told him that he would make Abraham into a great nation:

> I will make of you a great nation,
>   and I will bless you,
> and make your name great,
>   so that you will be a blessing.
> I will bless those who bless you,
>   and the one who curses you I will curse;
> and in you all the families of the earth
>   shall be blessed.

Genesis 12:2-3

56

God also promised Abraham a child to be his heir. St. Paul comments favorably: "Abraham believed God and it was reckoned to him as righteousness" (Rom. 4:3). The picture painted here is inspiring, yet one must wonder if it is the whole picture concerning Abraham's dealings with God. Let us flesh out this picture. After receiving this grand promise of blessing the nations through Abraham, the father of our faith lied twice to foreign kings in order to spare his own life, claiming that his beautiful wife was his sister and allowing them to sleep with her (Gen. 12:10-20; 20:1-18). Abraham believed God. Rather than patiently wait for a child from his own wife, as the Lord had promised, he slept with his servant, Hagar, and she conceived and bore a child called Ishmael (Gen. 16). Abraham believed God. When God appeared to Abraham again and told him that he would have a child through Sarah, his ninety-year-old wife, he fell down laughing in unbelief. God told Abraham and Sarah to name the child Isaac — "he laughs" (Gen. 17:17-19). Abraham believed God.

But Abraham is the model of faith primarily for how he responded when God asked him to sacrifice his son Isaac. It is for passing this terrifying test of faith that Abraham is commended.

Kierkegaard on Abraham

Kierkegaard reflects on the nature of faith as exemplified in Abraham in *Fear and Trembling*.[1] Although Kierkegaard was a Christian, he writes under the pseudonym Johannes de Silentio, an unbeliever who attempts in vain to understand faith. He finds the Abraham story, and hence the nature of faith, attractive but incomprehensible. Through various scenarios, de Silentio tries to imagine the thoughts of Abraham

1. Søren Kierkegaard, *Fear and Trembling,* and *The Sickness Unto Death,* trans. with intro. and notes by Walter Lowrie (Princeton: Princeton University Press, 1954).

as he goes off to Mount Moriah to sacrifice his only son. These speculations remind us that this "beautiful story" intends to teach the incredible difficulty and terrifying responsibility of believing in God. We now consider it a beautiful story only because we already know how it ends. It is the ending that transforms the story from a nightmare for Abraham's fragile faith into a triumph of religious devotion.

Forget the ending — that God provides a sacrifice — and the story appears to be an unfolding tragedy of untold proportions. Abraham has been asked to kill his son "whom he loved" (as if we needed to be reminded of that), the child of promise. He has been asked to sacrifice the hope of future generations, the one through whom all the peoples of the earth will be blessed.

Imagine being Abraham on that fateful morning. He rises early, perhaps waking his wife. "Where are you off to so early, Abraham?" she asks. What could Abraham say? "To sacrifice our son"? And then he goes to Isaac, shakes the last clouds of sleep from his mind, and wakes him. "Morning, Daddy," Isaac says softly, reaching up for a hug and a kiss. "What are we going to do today, Daddy? Are you going to take me with you?" he says excitedly, thinking of this special time with his father. As Abraham loads up the donkey, Isaac's anticipation builds. They go off together and Isaac asks where they are going. What does Abraham tell him? Does he tell Isaac that they are going away so that Abraham can kill him? Does he lie to his son? Does he just maintain his sad silence in their last few moments together?

As they approach the mountain, Isaac notices the wood for the burnt offering as well as the knife, and he asks Abraham where the lamb is for sacrifice. Abraham tells him that God will provide the lamb and proceeds to plot Isaac's doom. He ties Isaac down. "Why are you tying me, Daddy? Is this some sort of game?" Then he raises the knife. "What's the knife for, Daddy?" What does Abraham say? What could he be thinking?

We should not read the story too quickly; we shouldn't rush to learn how everything turns out. That is a luxury not afforded

Abraham. He does not know how the story will end. He does not know that God will provide a sacrifice that will prevent his killing Isaac. He raises the knife, sun glinting off its shiny blade, ready to plunge it into Isaac's heart.

Because of its familiarity, the story has lost its awesome power. So de Silentio considers various tellings of the story to help him understand the nature of faith. Kierkegaard uses de Silentio's speculations to rescue its radical truth from our insensitive ears. Perhaps, de Silentio wonders, Abraham explained to Isaac that he was about to be sacrificed:

> And Abraham's face was fatherliness, his look was mild, his speech encouraging. But Isaac was unable to understand him, his soul could not be exalted; he embraced Abraham's knees, he fell at his feet imploringly, he begged for his young life, for the fair hope of his future, he called to mind the joy in Abraham's house, he called to mind the sorrow and loneliness.[2]

Although Abraham attempts to comfort Isaac, he cannot be comforted with a knife poised to plunge into his heart. He looks into his father's face with horror and calls upon God as Father. Abraham takes the blame so that Isaac does not curse the God who has called Abraham to this action.

Perhaps Abraham silently and reluctantly followed God's command and at the last minute was rewarded with the substitute ram. But "he could not forget that God had required this of him. Isaac throve as before, but Abraham's eyes were darkened, and he knew joy no more."[3]

Perhaps Abraham was ravaged by the moral dilemma that God's command had posed between his duty to his son and his duty to God. As he rode to Mount Moriah "he threw himself upon his face, he prayed to God to forgive him his sin, that he had been willing to offer his son

2. Kierkegaard, *Fear and Trembling,* 27.
3. Kierkegaard, *Fear and Trembling,* 28.

Isaac, that the father had forgotten his duty toward the son." Yet he also thought that "it could not be a sin to be willing to offer to God the best thing he possessed. . . . For what sin could be more dreadful?"[4]

And finally, perhaps Abraham, just as he was about to plunge the knife into Isaac, despaired and Isaac noticed. The ram was provided, but Isaac lost his faith in God.

In each of these scenarios de Silentio cannot understand how Abraham persisted in faith. God commanded Abraham to depart from earthly wisdom and cling to faith. If we know anything about morality, we surely know that we should not kill our children. We should do all that we can do to protect them. Our hearts confirm this as well. Yet Abraham believed God and followed his commands without doubting; he embraced the incredible, that is, the unbelievable. What reasons could be given for sacrificing one's son? Abraham had to act when he could not understand — to walk by faith and not by sight. Johannes de Silentio cannot understand Abraham's faith because it cannot be understood; reason cannot resolve Abraham's dilemma. De Silentio wants to walk by sight and not by faith.

The author of Hebrews explains the nature of Abraham's faith in this way: "By faith Abraham, when put to the test, offered up Isaac. He who had received the promises was ready to offer up his only son, of whom he had been told, 'It is through Isaac that descendants shall be named for you.' He considered the fact that God is able to raise someone from the dead — and figuratively speaking, he did receive him back" (Heb. 11:17-18). This is the paradoxical faith of Abraham, and this is what de Silentio cannot fathom: *Abraham believed that he would kill his son and that he would get him back.* Abraham believed that Isaac would come back to life and that through him all the nations would be blessed. Abraham believed the unbelievable: he would give Isaac up and get him back. In spite of his prior peccadilloes of belief, when he was tested with the sacrifice of his son, he trusted God.

4. Kierkegaard, *Fear and Trembling,* 28-29.

the jolt of that fact

Because we are finite, there are very few matters about which we can attain certainty. While we long to prove, to the satisfaction of all serious inquirers, that God exists, that he is the foundation of morality, and that he is making us fit through his redemptive work for the next life, this is not possible. This lack of certainty is not impious; it is, rather, an expression of intellectual modesty. There is something odd about trying to prove that God became man, died for our sins, rose again from the dead on the third day, and has gone to prepare a room for us in the heavenly mansion. These are most peculiar beliefs.

David Hume, one of the Christian religion's most vaunted and powerful critics, wrote of the "miracle" of theism: Christian belief is so incredible that no reasonable person could assent to it without the aid of a miracle. While Christians have striven to demonstrate the reasonableness of their beliefs, they ought not understate the unnaturalness and apparent unreasonableness of their beliefs. As the apostle Paul contended, Christian beliefs are folly to the Greek and a stumbling block to the Jew (1 Cor. 1:23). They are rationally enigmatic and religiously problematic. Perhaps Hume was right.

Wouldn't it have been easier to believe, had we lived at the time of Jesus? If only we had seen Jesus and heard him speak, observed the healings and the miracles, and had the opportunity to follow him directly as did his disciples. Jesus' contemporaries, after all, could see him. We are expected to believe in Jesus almost two millennia after the fact, in an age of unbelief and uncertainty. If only we had been alive at the time of Jesus.

Then there is the scandal, which Jesus recognized and proclaimed, of believing in him. It was odd, even in Jesus' day, to believe that he was the Son of God. You could see Jesus the man; could you *see* the god part of him? Imagine living in his day, carefully and cautiously observing him, and then being asked to leave everything to follow the Son of God. What would you do? After all, he was a human being

61

like all of us — he ate and drank like the rest of us. He slept, laughed, and wept, needed his mother, and was once a mere baby who wet and soiled his cloak. It would be strange, even if you had seen Jesus, to believe that this man was also God.

If anyone were to make this audacious claim in our day, we would have him locked up in the nearest mental institution. Our natural reaction to human claims of divinity can be seen in our judgments concerning messianic claims made by and on behalf of contemporary figures like David Koresh or Sun Myung Moon. Prior to any additional information about the person's character or practices, we would form opinions about whether or not his claim to divinity was true. The natural reaction of reasonable people would be that the claim is ludicrous. This guy can't be God incarnate; he is only a human being. We have seen pictures of his parents, watched him walk and talk. Even if we were to spend time with the man, grow to enjoy his company and to be impressed with his teaching authority, it would still be reasonable to remain skeptical about his claim. If this is how we would react to someone claiming divinity today, why do we think it is so easy to believe this claim made by a man 2,000 years ago? Kierkegaard wants to confront us with the uncomfortable fact that this belief is neither easy nor natural. And it would not be any easier had we lived in the time of Jesus.

Kierkegaard challenges this wish to go back when belief in Jesus the Christ, God in the flesh, was supposedly easier. The contemporary of Jesus was simply closer "to the jolt of that fact." The twentieth-century believer has an advantage, in some ways: over the centuries it has become natural to believe that Jesus was God in the flesh; the scandal of the incarnation has ceased to amaze. I am often surprised at how few Christians are astounded, as they ought to be, by the claim that Jesus is God incarnate. Faith requires the extraordinary movement from believing that Jesus was more than just a wonderful, compassionate, and amazing man to believing that he was God in the flesh. Genuine faith requires that one experience the jolt of that fact and not simply hold a familiar belief that has been deprived of its power and scandal through the ages.

Consider, however, Jesus' followers — those who saw him, touched him, walked with him, and listened to him. Did they find it easy to believe? In John 6, when Jesus proclaims that he has been sent from heaven, many grumble: "Is this not Jesus, the son of Joseph, whose father and mother we know? How can he now say, 'I have come down from heaven?'" He claims to be the son of God, but we know who his parents are! He's the carpenter's son. The jolt of that fact. When Jesus claims that one must believe in him and eat his flesh to obtain eternal life, many of his own disciples grumble: "This teaching is difficult; who can accept it?" And many who had followed him for a long time could no longer believe: "Because of this many of his disciples turned back and no longer went about with him." The jolt of that fact.

the paradox of Christian belief

The final jolt, as Kierkegaard helps us recognize, is the incarnation itself. The incarnation calls us to embrace a set of beliefs that are difficult at best and, at worst, paradoxical and incoherent. Consider the properties that we typically ascribe to human beings and those we ascribe to God:

Humans	God
Limited in power	Omnipotent
Limited in space	Omnipresent
Limited in time	Eternal
Limited in knowledge	Omniscient

This list could be extended. To accept the incarnation, one must accept what Kierkegaard calls the absolute paradox — that in one person resides these apparently contradictory properties. The incarnation is at best an incomprehensible mystery and at worst an affront to reason. It is truly folly to the Greeks.

To believe as Abraham did, though, we must affirm this paradox; we must believe that Jesus is both fully God and fully human. As Abraham believed the apparent contradiction that he would kill his son and get him back, so too must we believe the apparent contradiction involved in the incarnation. *We must believe as Abraham.* The test of belief for us is like Abraham's test of faith. We are not being asked to kill our only son, but we are being asked to believe that God sacrificed his only son. And this is a hard teaching.

I teach a course on the meaning of life, in which I contrast the world view of the Christian with the world view of the atheistic existentialist. I carefully present the existentialist's pessimistic estimation of the possibilities for leading a significant human life. Sartre and Camus give a picture of the world that most of my Christian students find utterly distasteful and disheartening. My students cannot imagine living without the hope of redemption. They almost always wonder why those atheists who realize they are insignificant if there is no God don't simply believe in God as revealed in Jesus Christ. For them, Christian belief is as obvious as the air they breathe; they can't see air, but they know they depend on it for their existence. Why can't these obstinate atheists simply embrace the obvious? These students fail to understand the scandal of their own belief. Jesus Christ is fully God and fully human. They haven't been jolted by that fact.

fear and trembling

Nowadays, contrary to the lessons of the Abraham story, people treat faith as easily acquired and maintained, not as a lifelong process. Both intellectually and morally, we tend to downplay the genuine struggle of faith development. But as Kierkegaard writes: "In those old days it was different, then faith was a task for a whole lifetime, because it was assumed that dexterity in faith is not acquired in a few days or weeks."[5]

The erroneous nature of facile faith is manifest in Kierkegaard's ironic comparison between understanding Hegel, the monumentally difficult philosopher, and Abraham, the father of our faith: "It is supposed to be difficult to understand Hegel, but to understand Abraham is a trifle. To go beyond Hegel is a miracle, but to get beyond Abraham is the easiest thing of all."[6] Kierkegaard, of course, believes that it is infinitely more difficult to understand Abraham than to comprehend the impenetrable Hegel.

The resolution of doubt and the embracing of faith involve the entire individual, heart as well as mind. Commitment to the person of Christ entails much more than understanding and believing a set of propositions. Genuine faith involves the entire character of a person. Faith is a lifelong process of development that involves the complete transformation of the whole person. Fundamentally, it involves a terrifying and total denial of self. Kierkegaard derives the title of his book from Paul's sobering and serious injunction to "work out your own salvation with fear and trembling" (Phil. 2.12). Christian faith does not engender doubt merely because of the intellectual objections raised by modern atheism or the challenges posed by the paradoxes of Christian belief. Christian belief speaks not only to our mind, but also to our hearts. It proclaims a moral Lord of the universe who does not prize individual autonomy: "You are not your own; you were bought with a price" (1 Cor. 6:19-20). While we may desire and require forgiveness, we have little interest in surrendering our autonomy. God is not only lover, but also threat.

If the biblical portrait of humanity is correct, then we must advance from despising God to revering him to loving him. We may, out of self-interest, desire the benefits of belief in God, but our heart

5. Kierkegaard, *Fear and Trembling,* 23.
6. Kierkegaard, *Fear and Trembling,* 43.

of hearts rebels against the constraints imposed by the divine will. The process of faith is a lifelong struggle to learn to love God because he is good and worthy of our love and trust and not because he offers us benefits. Before we can proceed to genuine love of God, he must pierce the crust of self. Faith is a persistent threat to self. Until the last vestiges of our grasping and gasping ego are destroyed, faith will be simultaneously dangerous and inviting, dreadful and delightful.

The Christian, then, can never say with the rich man in the parable, "Soul, thou hast much goods laid up for many years, take thine ease." Total fellowship with God is not fully attainable in this earthly life. For Christians, there can be no genuine Sabbath, no final point of rest, until we have arrived at our ultimate destination. When our faith has withstood its tests, as Abraham's did, God will grant the Sabbath rest.

In 1987 the students at the Christian college where I taught carried on a heated debate, privately and in the school newspaper, about whether Bono, the lead singer of the rock group U2, was still a Christian. Although he had on many occasions publicly professed his faith, and while some of his songs contained explicitly Christian lyrics, many of the students doubted his commitment because of the lyrics of the song "I Still Haven't Found What I'm Looking For." The final verse was evidence of his alleged change of heart:

> I believe in the kingdom come
> When all the colors
> will bleed into one, bleed into one
> but yes, I'm still running.
> You broke the bonds
> And you loosed the chains
> Carried the cross and
> all my shame, all my shame
> You know I believe it
> But I still haven't found what I'm looking for.

66

What many students perceived as capitulation and unbelief is a poetic and potent modern expression of faith. Intertwined with his doubts is a profound commitment to Christ and a contemporary affirmation of the Kierkegaardian conception of faith as a lifetime struggle.

the journey of faith

So what is faith? What does it mean to believe if one is uncertain, on the basis of reason, that God exists and that Jesus is his son? One may still be committed to Jesus Christ even if one is uncertain. Faith is holding fast to Christ even while acknowledging that one might be wrong. The Christian walks by faith, not by sight.

Consider Jesus' disciples who stayed with him when other followers deserted. Did they persist because reason persuaded them that Jesus was the Christ? Did they remain because all their intellectual doubts had been removed and they alone were able to understand what the others could not: that Jesus, son of Mary and Joseph, was also the Son of God and that entrance to heaven could not be obtained without believing in him and eating his flesh? They held fast to Christ and continued to believe, in spite of many deep questions. When Jesus asked them if they wanted to leave too, Peter replied: "Lord, to whom can we go? You have the words of eternal life" (John 6:68).

The writer of Hebrews states that "faith is the assurance of things hoped for, the conviction of things not seen" (Heb. 11:1). The model of faith, as we have seen, is Abraham, who by faith obeyed God's calling "to set out for a place that he was to receive as an inheritance" (11:3). As the author of Hebrews writes of all the heroes of faith: "All these died in faith without having received the promises, but from a distance they saw and greeted them. They confessed that they were strangers and foreigners on earth . . . they desire a better country, that is, a heavenly one" (11:13-16). The writer of Hebrews suggests that faith is a journey, a pilgrimage to receive what is promised by God.

But Abraham and the rest do not see the inheritance; they carry within themselves only the promise made, not the promise fulfilled.

Scripture emphasizes hoping, yearning, and seeking for God more than attaining certain or infallible knowledge of God. Faith is a longing, a hoping, a desire to journey to the end and to find one's way back to fellowship with God and humans. Faith says, surely with some regret, "This world is not my home," and it seeks its true home. Faith involves a dissatisfaction with present realities and a hope for redemption.

Faith is a glimpse, a moment of insight when we see our future home and commit ourselves to completing the journey before twilight. Although we may not be intellectually convinced that this is indeed the right road, faith keeps our feet on the path.

the gift of faith

If we have restored power and passion to the Abraham story, then Kierkegaard has accomplished his task of reintroducing genuine faith to the Church. The incarnation of Jesus is nothing less than an offense to common sense. But it is precisely this uncommonness that makes it appealing — that Omnipotence in divine humility could appear as both compassionate lover and merciful judge and mingle with human flesh. God embraces his creation while simultaneously redeeming it. This is truly a message sent from God (for no human being in her right mind would have dreamed up this story!). The incarnation is an offense to reason, but one that makes its own peculiar sense.

It is also appealing because it satisfies fundamental, and otherwise irresolvable, human needs. We feel hopeless, aimless, alienated, and guilty. Our quest for a worthwhile life has led us to the recognition that we have not led a worthy life. We are stuck so firmly in sin that we scarcely recognize it in ourselves (although we are expert in recognizing it in others). What we need is a loving and forgiving relationship with our Creator and with others, but we lack both the will and the way. Intellect and will cannot lead us to God. Because we lack the means to save ourselves, we must accept faith as a gift. Desperately seeking forgiveness, we accept the embrace of God in Jesus Christ.

chapter 5

Hope and
Human Suffering

And thus our good Lord answered to all the questions and doubts which I could raise, saying most comfortingly in this fashion: *I will make all things well, I shall make all things well, I may make all things well and I can make all things well; and you will see that yourself, that all things will be well.*

And in these words God wishes to be enclosed in rest and in peace. And so Christ's spiritual thirst has an end. For his spiritual thirst is his longing in love, and that persists and always will until we see him on the day of judgment. Therefore his thirst is this incompleteness of his joy, that he does not now possess us in himself as wholly as he then will.

So he has pity and compassion on us and he longs to possess us, but his wisdom and his love do not permit the end to come until the best time. And in these same words said before: "I may make all things well," I understand powerful consolation from all the deeds of our Lord which are still to be performed; for just as the blessed Trinity created everything from nothing, just so the same blessed Trinity will make well all things which are not well. It is God's will that we pay great heed to all the deeds which he has performed, for he wishes us to know from them all which he will do; and he revealed that to me by those words which he said: And you will see yourself that every kind of thing will be well. I understand this in two ways: One is that I am well content that I do not know it; and the other is that I am glad and joyful because I shall know it.

Julian of Norwich, *Revelations of Divine Love*

ooooo

72

Suffering casts deep and dark shadows over our faith in a moral foundation of the universe and in a perfectly good, omnipotent deity. Many Christians vastly underestimate the kinds and amounts of evil in the universe, thereby diminishing the power of these problems. In addition, many Christians extol the excellencies of human suffering as God's warnings, calling us to repent and to allow God to carve out character in recalcitrant human material.

Suffering is a problem for sinner and saint alike. No deep religious conviction is untainted by the problem of human suffering. The most potent of faiths can be brought low by the swift blow of affliction. Our confidence can be shattered by the death of a child or by a natural disaster. How are we to maintain our faith in the face of human misery? Most solutions offer glib answers that are inadequate to the reality of suffering. We learn from Job that beyond the suffering that can be explained away as human punishment or divine warning or character forming lies more suffering. In the words of Yeats's haunting refrain: "The world's more full of weeping than we can understand."

In this chapter we will examine the problem of belief in God's existence and goodness in the face of human suffering. After raising the general problem, we will consider the book of Job — the most extended biblical treatment of the problem of human suffering. In the background of Job stands the traditional view that all suffering is punishment for human sin, which he painfully comes to reject. He has nothing to offer in its place and is left to suffer in silence, knowing neither its purpose nor its intended results. But God speaks to Job out of the whirlwind, and Job's face-to-face encounter with God provides a grounding for Job's hope that underneath all of this suffering there is a God who cares, who is determined that everything shall be made right, and who is able to make it so.

for goodness' sake?

The prologue of the book of Job raises this question: who will serve God without reward? Does it pay to serve God and, if not, why obey Him? The book describes Job as a good man — blameless, upright and God-fearing — who turned away from evil. God concurs with this description and is pleased with Job. But then Satan comes on the scene. Satan contends that Job is only faithful because God has blessed him so richly with a grand estate, perfect health, and a beautiful family. Take away all of Job's riches, Satan says to God, and he will curse you to your face. God has been duped, the cynical Satan claims, about the willing obedience of his most faithful follower.

The story of Job raises the perennial issues of the undeserved suffering of the weak and the righteous and the appropriate response to human suffering. All those who are struggling to be righteous but find themselves suffering — who want to know "Why?" — are fellow travelers with Job. The book of Job is not ultimately about a man named Job who walked on this earth some 2,500 to 3,000 years ago; it is about every person.

The story is familiar: Job's oxen, sheep, camels, servants, sons, and daughters are killed and his house is destroyed. Job's initial response is noble — he shaves his head, falls upon the ground and worships the Lord, exclaiming: "Naked I came from my mother's womb, and naked shall I return there; the LORD gave, and the LORD has taken away; blessed be the name of the LORD" (1:21). Job, God's faithful servant, endures these hardships in trust and obedience to God.

Although the Lord is noticeably proud that his servant Job is still blameless and upright, Satan presses his charge that people are only obedient because they are recipients of God's favor. So Satan increases the intensity of Job's suffering by afflicting him with excruciating physical ailments. At this point, Job's wife encourages him to curse God and die, but Job holds fast to his God — accepting both good and evil from his hand. "In all this Job did not sin with his lips" (2:10; see also 1:22).

This familiar story takes several twists and turns that test the common notion of Job's steadfastness and patience. His estate in ruins, his children dead, his body in torment, Job is visited by his friends Eliphaz the Temanite, Bildad the Shuhite, and Zophar the Naamathite, who kindly come to console and comfort him. And comfort they do, sitting with him in the mourning seat for seven silent days. Eventually they speak. Job's friends are committed to the traditional view of his day — the belief that all suffering is the retributive punishment of God. On this view, God punishes all wickedness, protects the weak, and rewards the righteous.

This traditional view attributes all human suffering to divine punishment for specific sins. Violation of the moral economy, so the view goes, carries with it characteristic punishments. In our day AIDS is seen as God's retribution against homosexuality, lung cancer as God's wrath on smokers, the destruction of Iraq as God's punishment of the new Hitler, Saddam Hussein, and the collapse of the Soviet Union as God's judgment on communism. As you sow, so shall you reap.

There seems to be a great deal of biblical support for the traditional view. The entire Deuteronomistic history, that account of Israel's rise and fall as a nation that runs from Joshua through 2 Kings, presumes that disaster is punishment for sin. The book of Proverbs also takes this view for granted. As stated in Proverbs 21:21, "Whoever pursues righteousness and kindness will find life and honor." Both sides of the retributive coin are seen in Proverbs 14:32: "The wicked are overthrown by their evildoing, but the righteous find a refuge in their integrity." All suffering is deserved because of unrighteousness in one's life.

The prophetic literature occasionally endorses this view in an even more radical fashion that seems to make God directly responsible for calamity. The prophet Amos, for instance, asks the rhetorical question: "Does disaster befall a city unless the LORD has done it?" (Amos 3:6). Isaiah 45:7 says, "I form light and create darkness, I make weal and create woe; I the LORD do all these things."

Throughout much of the Old Testament, there is a simplistic

tendency to look for human fault behind every woe. Although Psalms 1 and 2 are relatively late in their entry into the Bible, they are representative of this attitude. The author of Psalm 1, like Job's friends, believes in a divinely ordained system of justice in which the righteous are rewarded and the wicked are punished. All are repaid according to their deeds.

> Happy are those
> who do not follow the advice of the wicked,
> or take the path that sinners tread,
>   or sit in the seat of scoffers;
> but their delight is in the law of the LORD,
>   and on his law they meditate day and night.
> They are like trees
>   planted by streams of water,
> which yield their fruit in its season,
>   and their leaves do not wither.
> In all that they do, they prosper.
>
> The wicked are not so,
>   but are like chaff that the wind drives away.
> Therefore the wicked will not stand in the judgment,
>   nor sinners in the congregation of the righteous;
> for the LORD watches over the way of the righteous,
>   but the way of the wicked will perish.
>
> Psalm 1

Job's comforters, smitten with the traditional view, are certain that Job simply needs to repent. Job's initial response manifests the torment that this suffering engenders in his very soul. He curses the day of his birth and laments that life and light are granted to sufferers; he feels that it is better never to have been born. Job is afflicted most because he has lost the order and meaning his faith gave to life: why should he, a righteous man, suffer? A just world order has given way to an absurd moral universe.

One after the other, Job's comforters echo the traditional refrain — Job's suffering is due to his unrighteousness. Eliphaz the Temanite proclaims that only the wicked suffer (4:7-9). He states: "Think now, who that was innocent ever perished?" No one, he claims, not even the angels can be righteous before God (4:17-19). Bildad the Shuhite looks at it from the righteousness side of the coin: if you were righteous, as you claim, God would have rewarded you; the Almighty does not pervert justice (8:1-7). Because Job is suffering, he must be unrighteous, and his suffering must be punishment for his unrighteousness. Zophar contends that Job is a blasphemer and a secret sinner whose punishment is less than it ought to be (11:1-6). God is not capricious; only the guilty suffer, and since Job is suffering, he must by guilty. The traditional response assumes that behind all human suffering there is something good and beneficial: God's call to repentance. Job's comforters therefore extol the penitential merits of human suffering.

In a surprising reversal and parody of Psalm 8, Job asks:

What are human beings that you make so much of them,
that you set your mind on them,
visit them every morning
    test them every moment?
Will you not look away from me for a while,
    let me alone until I swallow my spittle?
If I sin, what do I do to you,
    watcher of humanity?
Why have you made me your target?
    Why have I become a burden to you?

7:17-20

"Don't you have anything better to do, God, than meddle with mere humans?" Why are our sins, concerning which Job is blameless, such a big deal to God? How can our wickedness affect Omnipotence? People often speak of God as if he needs our praise and obedience, as if he would be lacking something if we failed to pay him homage. But God is completely self-sufficient; his ego is not dependent on the meager responses of human beings. So, Job wonders, why is God making such a big deal out of my life? Couldn't the Lord of the Universe profitably spend his time on more important matters than meddling in the affairs of a lowly Son of Adam? God seems to Job more like a window peeper than Sovereign Lord.

calling God to account

Job believes that a mistake has been made. He is not wicked; he does not deserve to suffer. He despairs of clearing his own name and finally gets ticked off; he loses patience and calls God to account for his betrayal of justice. God has become his enemy, and he God's.

> He has kindled his wrath against me,
>   and counts me as his adversary.
> His troops come on together;
>   they have thrown up siege works against me,
> and encamp around my tent.
>
> 19:11-12

How does one protest one's innocence with God? Job is a righteous man and, given traditional beliefs, deserves to be rewarded, not punished. By Job's lights, God has really botched things up. Since God is clearly uninterested in setting Job's record straight, it is up to Job to set God straight. But how can a person contend with God? If God has all the power, then might makes right. Even though Job is innocent and God has bungled his dealings with him, Job cannot question God. God is the omnipotent judge — who can speak against him? Earlier in the cycle of speeches, Job says:

Though I am innocent, I cannot answer him;
I must appeal for mercy to my accuser.
If I summoned him and he answered me,
    I do not believe that he would listen to my voice.
For he crushes me with a tempest,
    and multiplies my wounds without cause;
he will not let me get my breath,
    but fills me with bitterness.
If it is a contest of strength, he is the strong one!
    If it is a matter of justice, who can summon him?
Though I am innocent, my own mouth would condemn me;
    though I am blameless, he would prove me perverse.

9:15-21

After lamenting the futility of appealing to God, Job accuses God of treating the innocent and the wicked alike:

It is all one; therefore I say,
    he destroys both the blameless and the wicked.
When disaster brings sudden death,
    he mocks at the calamity of the innocent.
The earth is given into the hand of the wicked;
he covers the eyes of its judges —
    if it is not he, who then is it?

9:22-24

God is the executive, legislative and judicial branches of the cosmos all rolled into one. Who has the power to contend with him? Even though Job is innocent (and the book never leads us to doubt this), God has the power to prove him guilty. God is the omnipotent accuser *and* judge. Who can win a case when the court is stacked like that? It is little wonder that Job feels utterly helpless. If it is a matter of justice, who can summon God?

Job simply wants to argue his case with God. But how can he

honestly speak as he pleases against God? His case is wholly unflattering to God, and God has the power to obliterate Job to avenge his name. Job would never get a fair trial. The world is unjust, and God seems a capricious despot. But Job is unafraid (the worst that could happen is that he could die, but he would welcome that). Even though God may annihilate him, at least he will have his say with the bully judge:

> But I would speak to the Almighty,
>> and I desire to argue my case with God. . . .
> See, he will kill me; I have no hope;
>> but I will defend my ways to his face. . . .
> I have indeed prepared my case;
>> I know that I shall be vindicated.
>
> 13:3, 15, 18

In order to take God to court, Job asks for God to become his equal — to give up the unfair advantage that his power grants him. Let God be judge, but not a bully, and then Job will have a fair day in court. Job the defendant will make his case before and against God the judge. When God and Job become more like equals, Job will be vindicated and God will be seen as capricious:

> Only grant two things to me,
>> then I will not hide myself from your face:
> withdraw your hand far from me.
>> and do not let dread of you terrify me.
> Then call, and I will answer;
>> or let me speak, and you reply to me.
>
> 13:20-22

God is a hidden God, and his absence denies Job the face-to-face encounter he desires. God has all the power and doesn't even need to show up to win. No one can stand up to God (even though he needs to be stood up to). Since God is the supreme judge, with all the power, no one can arbitrate between God and Job. But Job at least wants a chance to state his case, and he is certain that if given the chance he will be vindicated.

Job's vision of the world does not include a conscious life after death, and he believes that his hope may perish with him in the grave. He nevertheless believes that even if he dies, he will still be vindicated. In the words of Handel's *Messiah:*

> I know that my Redeemer liveth
> > and at last he will stand upon the earth.
> And tho' worms destroy my body,
> > yet in my flesh shall I see God.
>
> > > > > 19:25-26

This is typically taken as a profound statement of faith and trust on Job's part. But the hoped for redeemer is more likely an earthly vindicator who will clear Job's name in a face-to-face encounter with God. Even if Job dies, someone will take his case to the great high court and exonerate Job.

Job wants to find God and lay his case before him (23:3-7). He looks for God, but he is not there and cannot be found (23:8-9). "I cry to you and you do not answer me; I stand and you merely look at me. You have turned cruel to me; with the might of your hand you persecute me" (30:20-21). If Job were unrighteous, then God could justly punish him; but he is not. Therefore, God is doing Job an injustice. So, he makes his final challenge to his adversary. Job declares: "Let the Almighty answer me" (31:5).

out of the whirlwind

God speaks to Job out of the whirlwind. Job obtains at least part of what he demanded — an audience with God. But the roles are reversed: in the early chapters of the book, Job questions God and demands a reply, but now God questions Job and demands a reply.

81

The divine defense is a poetic description of God's mysterious and majestic power over nature. It paints a marvelous and occasionally terrifying picture of the wildness, beauty, and wonder of creation. God's reply never directly addresses Job's question about undeserved suffering, but his reply suggests that Job couldn't understand it. Job's meeting God face-to-face nevertheless allows him to see that God is good and powerful and in control of the world.

The Lord's first speech is a put-down that humbles Job. It exudes a sarcasm that seems intent on revealing to Job his puniness in this grand cosmos. God is great, so we are told, and Job correctly infers that he is exceedingly little.

> Who is this that darkens counsel by words without knowledge?
> Gird up your loins like a man,
>   I will question you,
>   and you shall declare to me.
> Where were you when I laid the foundation of the earth?
>   Tell me, if you have understanding.
> Who determined its measurements — surely you know!
>   Or who stretched a line upon it?
> On what were its bases sunk,
>   or who laid its cornerstone
> while the morning stars sang together,
>   and all the heavenly beings shouted for joy?
>
>   38:2-7

"Do you understand, Job," God continues, "the sea and its limits, the morning and the evening, death, the expanse of the earth, the dwelling of light, the storehouses of snow, the way of the stars or the wild ass?" We are as far from God, and understanding his ways, as a worm is from understanding us and our ways. The grand spectacle of God's creation reminds Job that he is not God, and it reinforces his own finitude and tininess. Job responds appropriately: "See, I am of small account; what shall I answer you?" (40:4). Then, reduced to silence, he places his hand over his mouth.

The picture of the world that God paints for Job is magnificent and beautiful. God's relationship to the world is a manifestation of his providential care. God orders the rising of the sun; arranges snow and hail to fall in times of trouble; supplies rain for our crops; carefully orders the seasons; controls lightening bolts; dispenses food to starving, infant ravens; watches tenderly as the doe bears her fawn; mirthfully makes ostriches with floppy, useless wings; fashions powerful, brave, and beautiful horses; and commands the eagle to soar into the heavens. Humans are not the only significant creatures in this picture; there is more to God's providential care than simply arranging matters for the benefit of human beings.

Job acknowledges the glory of the creation. He confesses that he has spoken of things "too wonderful" for him (42:3). God's work is too powerful and complex for Job to understand, but it is a good work, worthy of Job's awe, reverence, and praise. Job is humbled and silenced; God and his creation are glorified.

But there is a deep problem with the providential theme of which we should already be aware. God cares, we learn, for lions and lambs; but lions eat lambs. How is this a manifestation of providential care? God shows his concern for the lions and ravens by providing them with prey. But how does he show his concern for their prey? Of the soaring eagle, made to fly by the very power of God, we learn that "its young ones suck up blood, and where the slain are, there it is" (39:30).

What about the ostrich that lays its eggs in the warming sand "forgetful that a foot may crush them, and that a wild animal may trample them"?

It deals cruelly with its young, as if they were not its own;
   though its labor should be in vain, yet it has no fear;
because God has made it forget wisdom,
   and given it no share in understanding.   39:16-17

83

So God cares for darling does and cuddly fawns but not for witless ostriches and their young?

The very wonders of creation that make the morning stars rejoice have shifted into the terrifying. The creation is a grand and glorious place, but it is horrifying as well. Job reminds us that there is nothing so simple as the refrain "There's a wideness in God's mercy." He means to teach us a new refrain: "There's a wildness in God's mercy." As the Beaver tells us of Aslan, the Christ figure in C. S. Lewis's *The Lion, the Witch and the Wardrobe:* "'Course he isn't safe. But he's good. He's the King, I tell you."[1]

Annie Dillard recalls waking one morning and finding herself covered with her cat's bloody paw prints, looking as though she had been "painted with roses." Her comment on this experience makes clear the teachings of Job:

> What blood was this, and what roses? It could have been the rose of union, the blood of murder, or the rose of beauty bare and the blood of some unspeakable sacrifice or birth. The sign on my body could have been an emblem or a stain, the keys to the kingdom or the mark of Cain. I never knew. I never knew as I washed, and the blood streaked, faded, and finally disappeared, whether I'd purified myself or ruined the blood sign of the passover. We wake, if we ever wake at all, to mystery, rumors of death, beauty, violence. . . . "Seems like we're just set down here," a woman said to me recently, "and don't nobody know why."[2]

We wake, Job and Dillard remind us, if we ever wake at all, to mystery . . .

---

1. C. S. Lewis, *The Lion, the Witch and the Wardrobe* (New York: Macmillan, 1950), 76.

2. Annie Dillard, *Pilgrim at Tinker Creek* (New York: Harper's Magazine Press, 1974), 1-2.

omnipotence and human freedom

God also rejects Job's charge of injustice: "Will you even put me in the wrong? Will you condemn me that you may be justified?" (40:8). No attempt is made to justify Job's suffering through the traditional view of retribution. It is simply not true that all suffering is the divine repayment for evil. Indeed, God seems to imply that even divine omnipotence cannot solve the problem of human wickedness. Even if Job were to acquire the majesty of God, the problem of human suffering would still prove intractable. So God challenges Job, saying in effect: "I'd like to see *you* try to manage the world and deal with the wicked":

> Unleash the overflowings of your anger,
> and look on all who are proud, and abase them.
> Look on all who are proud and bring them low;
> tread down the wicked where they stand.
> Hide them all in the dust together;
> bind their faces in the world below.
> Then I will also acknowledge to you
> that your own right hand can give you victory.
>
> 40:11-14

If we step back and think about the implications of this passage, what can we say? Even though God is omnipotent, there is evil he cannot control *if he values the choices of free creatures.* If he allows genuinely free choices, with significant moral consequences, then both the righteous and the wicked will suffer. When God allows human beings to choose unrighteousness, not even omnipotence can guarantee that only the wicked will suffer.[3] After the story of the great flood, we are told that never again will God send a flood to wipe out human wickedness

---

3. See Kelly James Clark, *Return to Reason* (Grand Rapids: Eerdmans, 1990), 57-91.

(Gen. 9:11). Humans will be able to wreak havoc unimpeded. There will no longer be facile divine solutions to the problem of human wickedness and human suffering. God has determined not to intervene supernaturally to prevent holocausts, genocides, or the sufferings of innocents. God's willingness to let human events occur without divine intervention makes the humanly unthinkable possible.

We often make the claim that if we were God, we would never allow something like the Holocaust to happen. We would never tolerate wars, racism, and other evils. But we are not God, and we don't know the possibilities — the restrictions and the potentialities — that he faces when he decides to create free creatures. We also don't know what else God values and what other powers he struggles against in creating an arena for our moral and spiritual development. The writers of Job do not want us to feel sorry for God, but they do want to make us aware of the limits of human understanding. "If we were God" becomes a nonsensical, silly statement that is unworthy of serious consideration. There is more to the governing of the world than meets the eye, and mere human beings are scarcely capable of plumbing the unfathomable and mysterious depths of divine wisdom.

What are the benefits of human freedom? God does not wish to make puppets, because he wants people to choose freely to love and obey him. But what are the costs? Is it so clear that the benefits of free will outweigh the costs? Is freedom a sufficiently great good to outweigh the costs of the suffering of all humanity? If so, why doesn't God just tell this to Job? Job seems clever enough to understand. The free-will theodicy, which is so popular among philosophers and theologians, fails to explain all the wickedness and human suffering that there is in the world. God is telling Job that much more is at stake — but what? This we are not told. We awake again to mystery.

suffering that is honest to God

After the speeches of God comes Job's final reply (42:1-6). He affirms God's omnipotence, confesses his lack of understanding, and repents in dust and ashes. In the epilogue (42:7-17), God castigates Job's friends and restores Job's fortune by doubling it. So we come back to where the book started, but we still do not know why the wicked prosper and the innocent suffer. Job's charges have not been answered. Yet he retracts his accusations and leaves his ash heap. As an intellectual explanation of the problem of human suffering, the book of Job is extremely unsatisfactory and disappointing. Job's probing questioning is met by a gigantic display of divine power. Job's worst fears seem realized when omnipotence bullies him into submission.

I believe that the Satan character is right—stripped of his possessions and earthly security, Job curses God. It was easy for Job to trust in God when he had it all—family, friends, vast wealth. But divested of his comforts and wrapped in affliction, Job comes to believe that God is not good and is, in fact, a chaos monster with little else to do than torment feeble humans. God asked Job, "Would you condemn me to justify yourself?" And that is precisely what Job has done: his bitterness blossoms into blasphemy.

So what does Job learn from his encounter with God that allows him to leave his ash heap and trust in God? Is it sheer fear of God's magnificent display of power? Has he come to a new understanding enabling him to reconcile God's power and goodness with his horrific suffering? What does he learn from this awesome, yet intellectually unsatisfying, epiphany? Job has gotten his wish—he has seen God face-to-face: "I had heard of you by the hearing of the ear, but now my eye sees you" (42:5). What Job has seen is not only an unparalleled display of divine power, but also a communication of divine grace. He has seen not only God's power but also his goodness. His admission of ignorance now—"I have uttered what I did not understand, things too wonderful for me, which I did not know" (42:3)—is no longer unacceptable because he has given up his presumption. Although he still does not understand why innocents suffer, he is embraced by the divine love, and his ignorance no longer poses an obstacle to his faithfulness. He has seen God's power and mercy, and in humility he trusts in God.

Why is the impudent and blaspheming accuser, Job, granted a divine audience while God's pious defenders are rebuked? Of Job's friends, God says: "You have not spoken of me what is right, as my servant Job has" (42:7). Job has both praised God and cursed him. He has spoken truly of God's sovereignty and power, his invincibility, his irresistibility, and his hiddenness. He has also seen clearly that God does not administer justice according to the traditional retributive view. His very life has counted as evidence against the view that only the wicked perish. And he has spoken honestly to God — he has thrown his anger and bitterness upon God. Only bitter, truth-speaking Job has spoken rightly and seen God face-to-face.

In *Holy the Firm*, Annie Dillard describes a pastor in a church she once visited:

> The man knows God. Once, in the middle of the long pastoral prayer of intercession for the whole world — for the gift of wisdom to its leaders, for hope and mercy to the grieving and pained, succor to the oppressed, and God's grace to all — in the middle of this he stopped, and burst out, "Lord, we bring you these same petitions every week." After a shocked pause, he continued reading the prayer. Because of this, I like him very much.[4]

Dillard's candid and courageous minister has learned the lesson of Job — to speak truly and honestly to God.

The Psalms of lament formed part of the communal worship of the ancient Hebrews, but many contemporary Christians often regard

---

4. Annie Dillard, *Holy the Firm* (New York: Harper and Row, 1977), 57-58.

them as impious or too negative. Far from being expressions of un-belief or marks of a lack of faith, the lament Psalms are signs of a community faithfully communing with their God. All of human ex-perience, even the most profound, finds expression in the Psalms. To repress the anxiety caused by human suffering is to fail to share one's deepest concerns with one's loving covenant partner. Conversation and fellowship with God demand complete and heartfelt honesty. It would have been unthinkable to the ancient Hebrews to withhold their secret longings and desires from the Lord. It is a sign of their trust that they could unburden their heavy hearts on the Lord of the universe. Withholding lament betrays a lack of fidelity. When we express our anguish to God, we draw God into our experience. To avoid God stoically in times of suffering or to maintain piously that "all is well" when we know good and well that it isn't — this prevents God from fully entering into our believing experience. The life of authentic faith demands raging at God when we want to know "Why?"

Job is offered not only God's message but also God himself. Part of the message of Job is that we needn't suffer impassively. We can even thrust our anger upon God. Our hope is that, as for Job, God will meet us with his grace. Many Christians think it is inappropriate to express their anger and frustrations to God. So they express only their happy thoughts to God and others. When I want my daughter to stop crying, I often entice her with treats and tell her that I will reward her when she is a happy girl. Instantaneously, if she prizes the reward, a noticeably fake smile will break through the tears as she claims: "I'm a happy girl now, Daddy." Of course, she is only acting happy because she thinks that is what I want. And that is exactly how many of us relate to God — we hide our tears behind a fake smile, and all the while God knows how we really feel. We think we honor God with our false praise, but we don't. God is big enough and cares enough to bear our anger. God graciously meets the blasphemer with a vision of his power and good-ness. And when we, like Job, receive this healing balm, we no longer need to find completely rational answers.

glimmers of hope

At stake for Job are God's power and, above all, his goodness. Job's experience of God provides a grounding for his hope that God is indeed good and cares for his world. In addition to humility, Job gains grounds for trust in God. He is not yet persuaded by reason, but he can rest his trust and life in God himself. This provides a grounding for his hope that underneath apparent chaos is divine care. And it is precisely this hope that transforms Job's anxious questioning into trust.

In the film *Sophie's Choice*, the title character is sent to a Nazi concentration camp where she is forced to make a cruel decision. Sophie is the mother of two children, and a Nazi soldier forces her to make an unthinkable choice — which of her two children she will keep and which she will send away to die in the gas chamber. Any parent will feel viscerally the agony of making such a choice. My immediate reaction to the dilemma was that the Gestapo officer who forced her choice should pay for it. It was my hope that he would not get away with his wickedness.

In the film, however, the officer doesn't get punished. We ought to hope for a moral order of the universe in which he does. If justice isn't served in this life, we ought to hope for an afterlife where it is. We ought to hope that at its most fundamental level the universe will prove just. We ought to hope that suffering and death are not the last words.

Many atheists respond to evil in the world by struggling against evil. Theists should struggle too, but they should also hope. The world the atheist sees — full of evil and suffering but *without hope* — is infinitely more bleak than the world inhabited by the theist. Imagine the victims of the Holocaust unavenged. Imagine Hitler and Stalin unpunished and Mahatma Gandhi and Mother Teresa unrewarded. Such a world is a truly nightmarish world. If death is the last word, then this is the worst of all possible worlds. We ought to hope that ultimate reality is just, that the horrendous wrongs of this world will

90

be righted, and that our struggles and sufferings will not have been
in vain.

Even more we ought to hope that at the bottom of ultimate reality
is mercy. We are as much victimizers as victims, guilty as innocent.
I am more like the officer in the Nazi concentration camp than I am
like Jesus. We ought, therefore, to hope in mercy.

Our hope for a universe that is ultimately just does not mean that
the trust we place in God is blind. Consider Job again. Job doubted
neither God's existence nor his power but his goodness. In the dramatic divine encounter, he sees God face-to-face. He *sees* that God is
powerful and merciful. Job repents and returns to God because he has
been shown God's goodness and power.

The Christian is in a similar position. God has demonstrated both
his power and goodness through the death and resurrection of Jesus
Christ. God entered history to suffer with us and to redeem us.
Christians believe that, through Christ, the entire creation will return
to shalom, wholeness. We see in Jesus what Job saw in his divine
encounter — God's awesome power and mysterious goodness.

Beliefs alone can never make Christians confident of God's justice.
That confidence comes only when Christians experience forgiveness
and moral transformation and when they see broken lives made whole
in communities of faith that are themselves instruments of redemption. Belief and experience together confirm God's merciful power.
Being part of a redeemed and redemptive community provides
grounds for believing that God, in manifold and mysterious ways, is
actively bringing good out of evil and will one day complete this
project. The Church reenacts key events of redemptive history in her
liturgy — Advent, Christmas, Easter, and the Lord's supper. Apparently answered prayers, occasional signs of divine providence, and
a sense of peace in the midst of trials and tribulations lend credence
to the Christian's belief that God is redeeming the world with compassionate power.

In the incarnation God manifests the power of his compassion,

91

his willingness to suffer with us, his desire and ability to redeem. The model of divine love is manifested in the Exodus — God knows our suffering, hears our cries, and has come to rescue us. God redeems us by sharing in our sufferings. It is through his suffering that all suffering is — will be — redeemed. Jesus' ultimate redemptive task was to conquer sin by accepting suffering. He meets suffering with suffering love. He invites his disciples to participate in this redemptive process, to drink the cup of suffering, and to take up the cross and follow him. Compassionate suffering will win out in the end.

Against the bricks and bullets of wickedness in this world, Jesus calls us to be gentle, compassionate, and patient. We are to suffer with him by being like him in his battle against sin, death, and the Devil. God's victory was gained by compassion, not coercion. The Suffering Servant becomes a model for our lives. Even while we cannot understand evil, we must work to redeem it. We are called to participate in the redemptive process. Like Christ, we must be compassionate healers — dealers in life, not in death. Of course, our compassion alone is no match for the horrific power of evil. We must hope that God's is.

chapter 6

Help Thou
Mine Unbelief

Perplext in faith, but pure in deeds,
　　At last he beat his music out.
　　There lives more faith in honest doubt,
Believe me, than in half the creeds.

Tennyson, In Memoriam

I think there is no suffering greater than what is caused by the doubts of those who want to believe. I know what torment this is, but I can only see it, in myself anyway, as the process by which faith is deepened. A faith that just accepts is a child's faith and all right for children, but eventually you have to grow religiously as every other way, though some never do.

What people don't realize is how much religion costs. They think faith is a big electric blanket, when of course it is a cross. It is much harder to believe than not to believe. If you feel you can't believe, you must at least do this: keep an open mind. Keep it open toward faith, keep wanting it, keep asking for it, and leave the rest to God.

When we get our spiritual house in order, we'll be dead. This goes on. You arrive at enough certainty to be able to make your way, but it is making it in darkness. Don't expect faith to clear things up for you. It is trust, not certainty.

Flannery O'Connor, The Habit of Being

But there are hours, and they come to us all at some period of life or other, when the hand of Mystery seems to be heavy on the soul — when some life-shock scatters existence, leaves it a blank and dreary waste henceforth forever, and there appears nothing of hope in all the expanse which stretches out, except that merciful gate of death which opens at the end — hours when the sense of misplaced or ill-requited affection, the feeling of personal worthlessness, the uncertainty and meanness of all human aims, and a doubt of all human goodness, unfix the soul from its old moorings, and leave it drifting, drifting over the vast infinitude, with an awful sense of solitariness. Then the man whose faith rested on outward authority and not on inward life will find it give way . . . — God — will be an awful desolate Perhaps. Well in such moments you doubt all — whether Christianity be true: whether Christ was man or God or a beautiful fable. You ask bitterly, like Pontius Pilate, What is Truth? In such an hour what remains? I reply, Obedience. Leave those thoughts for the present. Act — be merciful and gentle — honest; force yourself to abound in little services; try to do good to others; be true to the duty that you know. *That* must be right, whatever else is uncertain. And by all the laws of the human heart, by the word of God, you shall not be left in doubt. Do that much of the will of God which is plain to you, and "You shall know of the doctrine, whether it be of God."

F. W. Robertson, *Sermons*

A few years ago I was surprised to learn that my nine-year-old niece still believed in Santa Claus. I asked my mother-in-law if she was sure about this. She replied that my niece never questioned Santa's existence because she was afraid that if she did, she might no longer receive any presents from him. This seemed to me to capture the reluctance of Christians to express their doubts. Many Christians have deep misgivings about manifesting doubt because they fear that

God will deny them his presents. So doubt is repressed rather than expressed. Why do we choose to relate to God as a child to Santa?

What is the meaning of faith in a life distinguished by doubt? How are we to relate properly to a divine being of whose existence we are not intellectually certain? Does God answer our prayer "Help thou mine unbelief"?

making do with doubt

The Christian self-help manuals offer ten steps that, if fastidiously followed, will guarantee that prayers will move mountains: your business will prosper, your children will grow up beautifully, you will find yourself effortlessly applying Scripture to every area of your life, and you will become a giant of faith. The manuals treat doubt as one would a headache, a broken arm, or athlete's foot. Simply following the doctor's orders, applying the quick remedy, or popping a pill will relieve both symptoms and malady. But doubt is really more like arthritis, nearsightedness, and the common cold. These are not necessarily terminal ailments, but they are not easily curable either. Some of their symptoms can be masked for a while, but sooner rather than later they manifest themselves, sometimes quite powerfully. These are ailments we must simply learn to live with, even though learning to live with them is not something we desire or welcome. So too with doubt: it is a malady that we shouldn't relish or glorify, but we must make do with it.

the divided self

John Calvin, the Reformed theologian, writes of a convinced and certain faith, of belief without wavering.[1] However, he quickly proceeds to add:

1. John Calvin, *Institutes of the Christian Religion*, trans. Henry Beveridge (Grand Rapids: Eerdmans, 1975).

Still, someone will say: "Believers experience something far different: In recognizing the grace of God toward themselves they are not only tried by disquiet, which often comes upon them, but they are repeatedly shaken by gravest terrors. For so violent are the temptations that trouble their minds as not to seem quite compatible with that certainty of faith." Accordingly, we shall have to solve this difficulty if we wish the above-stated doctrine to stand. Surely, while we teach that faith ought to be certain and assured, we cannot imagine any certainty that is not tinged with doubt, or any assurance that is not assailed by some anxiety. On the other hand, we say that believers are in perpetual conflict with their own unbelief. Far, indeed, are we from putting their consciences in any peaceful repose, undisturbed by any tumult at all. (*Institutes,* 3.2.17)

How can he write both that our faith must be certain and yet that it will always be tinged with doubt? He seems torn between the biblical demand for certainty and the experiential obviousness of doubt. He unpacks the believer's dilemma in this way:

In order to understand this, it is necessary to return to that division of flesh and spirit which we have mentioned elsewhere. It most clearly reveals itself at this point. Therefore the godly heart feels in itself a division because it is partly imbued with sweetness from its recognition of the divine goodness, partly grieves in bitterness from an awareness of its calamity; partly rests upon the promise of the gospel, partly trembles at the evidence of its own iniquity; partly rejoices at the expectation of life, partly shudders at death. This variation arises from imperfection of faith, since in the course of the present life it never goes so well with us that we are wholly cured of the disease of unbelief and entirely filled and possessed by faith. Hence arise those conflicts; when unbelief, which reposes in the remains of the flesh, rises up to attack the faith that has been inwardly conceived. (*Institutes,* 3.2.18)

While Calvin sees perfection in belief, faith without doubt, as a goal for which Christians ought to hope and towards which they ought to strive, he refuses to downplay the inevitable doubts believers face. Our divided hearts and minds are a constant and conflicting fount of delight and dread.

Scripture itself, though, seems at times to downplay the reality of doubt in the life of a genuine believer.

> If any of you is lacking in wisdom, ask God, who gives to all gener-ously and ungrudgingly, and it will be given you. But ask in faith, never doubting, for the one who doubts is like a wave of the sea, driven and tossed by the wind; for the doubter, being double-minded and unstable in every way, must not expect to receive anything from the Lord. (James 1:5-8)

Most people are willing to admit that no one in this life will attain moral perfection. Although we are often judgmental of others' short-comings and too eager to rationalize our own, we recognize that the Christian life does not automatically engender perfection in virtue. When Jesus calls us to be perfect as he is perfect, we properly under-stand this as a goal to be attained through a lifetime of moral struggle. So the Christian life is goal-directed — we are to become children of God, heirs of eternal life. But we are now, it seems, infinitely far from that goal. In our moral shortcomings, we trust and hope that God will grant us mercy and not justice.

We fall far short of the goal in our behavior and in our believing. We are no more perfect in belief than we are in virtue. I don't mean to suggest that we ought to give up striving for belief without doubt or abandon the quest for moral perfection. But we must reckon with the reality that, in this life, our attaining perfection in belief is as unlikely as our attaining perfection in practice. Falling short of these goals is not praiseworthy. But doubt, like sin, is an ever-present reality in our earthly life; we should face it honestly.

98

doubters welcome

So many Christians seem to demand perfection in belief and speak of their unshakable conviction. What do they have that we doubters don't? In this mortal life, belief and unbelief reside in the same person just as righteousness and wickedness do. We need, therefore, to deal with one another in belief as God deals with us in our sin — with mercy.

Everyone, both the stout of faith and the infirm in belief, should be part of a caring community. We should never believe or doubt entirely on our own. I remember a close friend in college who had profound doubts about both God's existence and his own salvation. We were part of a Bible study that disavowed doubt. A little booklet entitled *Doubters Welcome* was passed around in the group. The booklet ironically communicated the real values of the fellowship — doubters were not really or fully welcome. Doubt was considered a condition that plagued unbelievers, and only when one was relieved of this condition could one properly take one's place in the group. The group became a place for the already healed, not for those struggling to find the cure. So my honest friend was looked upon with derision, treated as an outsider, and considered somewhat pathological in his failure of faith. "Come back when you are healthy" is the message he got.

We should understand that people are only partially sanctified in belief and should provide sympathetic care and support to those who honestly express their doubts. We shouldn't look on doubters with pity or derision but consider them fellow strugglers on life's way. We should pray not only that we may become good parents, get good grades on exams, get along with our employers and spouses, and see justice and peace prevail in this broken world, but also that the faith of our deeply divided souls may be strengthened.

I am speaking here of the doubt that comes from belief, not the doubt of unbelief. This doubt is endemic to religious belief and is distinguished from obstinate unbelief. The Bible, when it speaks of unbelief, refers to a hardness of heart, a stubbornness, an unwillingness to trust or hope in God. The sincere doubt of believers is quite different: it is the authentic expression of anguish over our wretched believing condition, and it includes a deep desire for and love of the truth. The doubt of indifference can be distinguished from the doubt that cares and seeks and hopes to find. To those who are indifferent, nothing is pledged. But those who search, it is promised, shall find.

This is where Doubting Thomas gets a bad rap. When he asks for signs from the risen Jesus he is told: "Blessed are those who have not seen and yet have come to believe" (John 20:29). "Blessed," of course, means "happy," and surely people who blithely remain faithful without need of proof *are* happy. But God has given us inquiring minds, and some of us cannot be at peace in our beliefs until our minds are at rest. Jesus does not turn Thomas away; his reply is not a rebuke. The doubt of Thomas is one that cares deeply for the truth, that wants desperately to find the true way. Jesus gives him what he asks for and relieves the burden of his uncertainty: "Put your finger here and see my hands. Reach out your hand and put it in my side. Do not doubt but believe" (John 20:27). Thomas sincerely sought and found.

Scripture tells of God's faithful love in the midst of our faithlessness: "A bruised reed he will not break, and a dimly burning wick he will not quench" (Isa. 42:3; Matt. 12:20). We should model God's patient and steadfast love in our dealings with doubters. This means honestly recognizing the lack of certainty in all of our lives. We should be the last to snuff out the smoldering wick of faith. We should be willing to pray for and support doubting brethren. We should never cast the first stone, but embrace those who have been assailed even by pebbles of doubt.

testing the mettle of faith

It is ironic that, along with tremendous reduction in human suffering, modern science has eroded religious belief. Although people now live

100

longer, healthier lives, they find it more difficult to believe in God. Our spiritual ancestors took suffering as a test; through it their faith was made complete (even now faith seems strongest in countries that are economically destitute or where political forces are aligned against religious belief). I don't long for the days when faith was made strong by strife, but I do wonder sometimes what has happened to faith in our time. Perhaps it is through doubt instead of suffering that our faith is being made complete.

It is not only to the suffering that belief comes difficult. In times of earthly gain, we can find ourselves distant from God. Is God ignoring us, or are we ignoring him? Success at work, school, or play can create the false sense that we don't need God, that we are in control and doing fine, thank you very much. As we self-satisfyingly fill up our lives with our own accomplishments, we leave little room for God. In this situation, doubt can play a beneficial role: it can make us aware of the great good that we lack yet desperately need.

In his poem *In Memoriam,* Tennyson commends "the faith, the vigour bold, to dwell / On doubts that drive the coward back." Unsure whether or not doubt comes from the Devil, he nonetheless believes that doubt is a fire that tests the mettle of faith. "There lives more faith in honest doubt, / Believe me, than in half the creeds." Honest doubt, bravely faced, can become a training ground for the soul to develop a genuine and mature faith: "To find a stronger faith his own."

God's garage

Christians beset with debilitating doubt should act on what they do believe. Pascal's famous wager concludes that it makes sense to bet that God exists. But placing a wager and actually believing in God's existence are very different matters. Since your beliefs are not always within your conscious or direct control, Pascal suggests that if you want to become a believer, you should do the things that believers do:

101

You would like to attain faith, and do not know the way; you would like to cure yourself of unbelief, and ask the remedy for it. Learn of those who have been bound like you, and who now stake all their possessions. These are people who know the way which you would follow, and who are cured of an ill of which you would be cured. Follow the way by which they began; by acting as if they believed, taking the holy water, having masses said, etc. Even this will naturally make you believe.[2]

Pascal suggests this approach because he believes that the primary obstacle to religious faith is posed by the passions, not the intellect. Unbelievers, he contends, don't need an increase of proofs for their intellect; they require a decrease in the influence of the passions on their will. By following the religious practices of those who are availing themselves of the means of grace, one can diminish the effect of the passions on one's will. This may open the way for one to receive the gift of faith.

When I was on the staff of Young Life, I often heard and even used the following illustration about the importance of making a personal decision for Christ: "Going to church and doing good things won't make you a Christian. Sitting in a holy place will not make you holy. That would be like thinking that sitting in a garage long enough will make you into a car!" I have come to believe that this illustration is at least partly misleading. God *has* ordained means through which his grace is transmitted: preaching and hearing Scripture, reading and delighting in the book of nature, breaking bread and enjoying fellowship together, praying and worshipping together. Sitting in a church *can* prepare you to experience the love of God because it can put you in touch with the means of grace. So my advice for doubters is: Park yourself in God's garage! Obey what you can, avail yourself of the means of grace, and search for glimpses of light.

2. Blaise Pascal, *Pensées,* trans. W. F. Trotter (New York: E. P. Dutton, 1958), 68.

tips for travelers

So what can we do, we who are condemned to wander about in caves? How shall we find our way in the darkness with only glimmers of light? What is to prevent us from bumping into the walls and ceilings, tumbling down steep inclines, sliding uncontrollably on the ice, inhaling noxious gases, being consumed by explosions, crushed by collapsing ceilings, or falling down hidden shafts to our death? This much at least seems clear: given our human limitations, we are more likely to go wrong than right.

But follow the light we must. What other options are there? The lights may be dim, but they are lights, and we must follow them. However faint and frail they may be, they are all we have to direct our paths. In our fumbling, frantic search for wisdom, we must grasp onto what we can. If the only path we see is indistinct, indirect, or only partly illuminated, we must still take it.

Sometimes it is our social and cultural conditioning that poses obstacles to belief in God's existence and goodness. We are born into families that are spiritually, racially, and ethnically constituted. We are part of cultures that assume values and truths that we take to be self-evident. We are indoctrinated into sets of religious beliefs (whether Christian, Muslim, Buddhist, or atheist) virtually from the womb. We develop decided tastes for the sensory or the rational or the spiritual. Our experiences, upbringing, genetics, moral and spiritual education, and cultural conditioning have carved out a manageable cavity of plausibilities in the immense mountain of possibilities. By the time we reach the age of reflection, we have a drastically limited view of reality and its potentialities. We are trapped in a cave of social and cultural making, with no visible means of escape.

One option we have in dealing with our situation is skepticism. We can simply despair of our ability to find truth. We can set our butts down and refuse to go in any direction. There is no reason to prefer one path to another, the skeptic contends. But this attitude fails to see that deciding not to take one path simultaneously entails a decision to take (or stay on) another. In real life, we are all on one path or another. If one chooses the path of agnosticism rather than choosing a path that leads in a theistic direction, then one has indeed made a choice. If one chooses the way of atheism, one assumes all of the risks of that path. Skepticism does not allow one to avoid the risks; it simply embraces one set of risks rather than another. There is precious little comfort in skepticism.

A second option is relativism or pluralism — whatever path you take is the right path for you; truth is relative to time, place, circumstance, and personal inclination. All paths lead to God, the pluralist claims. The relativist option removes the urgency of exploring the cave. There are no missteps because, on this view, there are no wrong paths. There is, however, a problem with this option: some paths logically exclude other paths. They can't all be right. If one person says it is essential to follow path X and another that it is essential to avoid path X, they can't both be right. And that is exactly what competing religions claim. They make essential but contradictory claims about the proper path to God. Some of these paths, though rich in tradition and sincerely followed by millions, must be wrong. There is too much comfort in relativism.

So our final option is to determine to stumble along as best we can, following those lights that God has placed along our paths. We must recognize our limitations and in humility accept God's gracious guidance along life's way. Taking this course of action assumes that there is something called Truth, but it recognizes that truth is sometimes darn hard to figure out. Such is the adventure and terror of life. We follow the lights as best we can. We accept as true what, given our best judgments, seems to us to be true. We stand ready and willing to criticize our comfortable beliefs as we receive more insight. We remain open to the possibility that we have wandered into a thicket and need to be redirected. Our hope is to continue following the clues into the arms of God. Choosing to follow a path makes faith precarious and risky. And so it is—there is no escaping it. This path, like all other paths, entails risk. Make no mistake about it: belief in God is risky business.

hints, guesses, and hope

I once discussed faith with a close friend who was reared in a Christian family. Some of his brothers and sisters were no longer believers, but other family members were pastors and Christian teachers. We discussed how such disparate stations of belief could be taken up by siblings raised in the same positive and compelling Christian home. I finally asked him if he was certain that Christianity is true, and he candidly replied: "I hope it's true." I have found his answer both revealing and instructive. It is revealing because underneath this affirmation of faith is an honest and sober confession of uncertainty. And it is instructive because it also manifests the centrality of hope to the Christian faith. The very element of confessed uncertainty allows for the possibility of faith and the vitality of hope.

Hope is a rather underrated virtue. We hear great pronouncements on faith and love but few on hope. *Hope is the deep longing for a future reality that is not clearly seen.* We hope our children will grow up educated and responsible; we hope for a cure for AIDS and cancer; we hope for a revitalization of the moral fiber of our country; we hope for a reduction in the budget deficit. And we hope that God's promises to redeem the world and our lives are not in vain. But our children may fall in with unsavory friends; AIDS and some forms of cancer may prove intractable; our country may grow more susceptible to the wiles of greed and pleasure; and politicians may never acquire the will to make the tough budget cuts. And the world may perish in a solar extinction, and we may die and become food for worms.

This much seems certain: without hope, the longed-for future reality will never be realized. If we give up on rearing our children or trying to cure AIDS, if we become cynical about our country and its politicians, things will not turn out as we desire. Our hopes are often necessary for the attainment of a better future. And our loss of hope may ensure our future's demise. Better to live with hope.

Of course, all the sincere hoping in the world cannot create a divine being who cares for us and wills our future redemption. We can hope against hope, but we cannot hope this caring, redeeming God into existence. But God has provided us with reasons for hope. He has given us light that directs us and illuminates our experience. Our directed experience itself becomes the vantage point from which we see the prospect of moral and spiritual progress and the ground upon which we pray that this progress will continue into the world-without-end. As the great Christian poet T. S. Eliot wrote:

> These are only hints and guesses,
> Hints followed by guesses; and the rest
> Is prayer, observance, discipline, thought and action.
> The hint half guessed, the gift half understood, is Incarnation.[3]

We follow the clues that God has placed for us, obeying where we ought, believing when we can, and submitting when we must.

---

3. T. S. Eliot, *Four Quartets* (London: Faber and Faber, 1944), 33.

part II

Searching
for My Self

'The length of our days is seventy years —
or eighty, if we have the strength;
yet their span is but trouble and sorrow,
for they quickly pass, and we fly away.
So teach us to number our days
that we may get a heart of wisdom.

Psalm 90:10-12

chapter 7

Sound
and Fury

Except an epitaph tell me who lies there, I cannot tell by the dust, nor by the epitaph know which is the dust it speaks of, if another have been laid before or after in the same grave. Nor can any epitaph be confident in saying here lies, but here was laid. For so various, so vicissitudinary is all this world that even the dust of the grave hath revolutions. As the motions of an upper sphere imprint a motion in the lower sphere other than naturally it would have; so the changes of this life work after death. And as envy supplants and removes us alive, a shovel removes us and throws us out of our grave after death. No limbec, no weighs can tell you, this is dust royal, this plebeian dust. No commissions, no inquisition can say, this is catholic, this is heretical dust. All lie alike.

John Donne, *Sermons*

To be blessed in death, one must learn to live.
To be blessed in life, one must learn to die.

Duplessis-Mornay, *Trewnesse of the Christian Religion*

We fat all creatures else to fat us, and we fat ourselves for maggots.

Hamlet 4.3.21-22

OOOOO

Not many people sit around thinking about the meaning of life, and few of us will ever take a pilgrimage to Tibet in search of enlightenment from an ascetic guru. Unless you earn your living as a philosopher, you probably don't spend your days trying to answer the big question: What's it all about? Most of us do, however, feel the force of the question at one time or another, posed in much more personal terms: What is the meaning of *my* life? Does *my* life have any point? Lots of things can drive us to ask this question. The boredom and tedium of our daily routines, the anger and depression that attend chronic illness, the loss of someone we love or something we hold dear, the envy we feel toward people who seem more happy and successful than we have ever been. These are a few of our least favorite things, but they thrust the question of life upon us whether we like it or not.

undermined

No thinkers in this century were more concerned with the question of the meaning of life than the French existentialists, Jean-Paul Sartre and Albert Camus. Camus raises the importance of the question:

> There is but one truly philosophical problem, and that is suicide. Judging whether life is or is not worth living amounts to answering the fundamental question of philosophy. . . . These are facts the heart can feel.
>
> If I ask myself how to judge that this question is more urgent than that, I reply that one judges by the actions it entails. I have never seen anyone die for the ontological argument. Galileo, who held a scientific truth of great importance, abjured it with the greatest ease as soon as it endangered his life. In a certain sense, he did right. That truth was not worth the stake. Whether the earth or the sun revolves around the other is a matter of profound indifference. . . .

On the other hand, I see many people die because they judge that life is not worth living. I see others paradoxically getting killed for the ideas or illusions that give them a reason for living (what is called a reason for living is also an excellent reason for dying). I therefore conclude that the meaning of life is the most urgent of questions. How to answer it?[1]

If the meaning of life is the most urgent of questions, why do so many pay it so little heed and, indeed, scoff at it? Is the meaning of life only a question for ivory tower philosophers or mountaintop gurus who have the luxury to contemplate apparent nonsense? People who attend to these questions are those who, through various experiences in life, have been forced to face the issue squarely and honestly. The meaning of life is not a completely intellectual issue, however; it is also a matter of *feeling*. Losing one's job, contracting a debilitating or terminal illness, experiencing the loss of a parent or child or a close friend, feeling the awful silence of God in a world full of apparently pointless suffering, getting to age forty or seventy and feeling that one hasn't accomplished anything of significance, looking at the chilly prospects of life upon nearing graduation, or simply growing older, losing one's hair, one's teeth, and finally one's wits. These sorts of experiences make one feel what the mind has chosen to ignore — the enormous prospects and burdens of life, the fragility of happiness, and the inevitability of death. While we perpetually try to focus on the good in life and to remain happy, these feelings force us to examine our place in the cosmos; they focus us, or rather they bring life into focus.

Camus writes of a man who killed himself five years after the devastating loss of his daughter. The experience of his daughter's death had *undermined* him — the ground under him had given way,

1. Albert Camus, *The Myth of Sysiphus and Other Essays*, trans. Justin O'Brien (New York: Knopf, 1958), 3.

the foundations had collapsed, the props had been removed. Death has a knack for making one look at life in a new and more honest way.

Lee Atwater, former Republican party chairman and engineer of George Bush's 1988 presidential victory over Michael Dukakis, lay dying of inoperable brain cancer. An unscrupulous campaigner, he masterminded, among many devious strategies, the racist Willy Horton advertisements alleging that Dukakis favored freeing (black) convicts. Atwater wanted it to appear, he admitted, as if Horton himself were Dukakis's running mate. Supremely gifted in intelligence, music, and political wisdom, he now lay in bed hoping to be able to walk again. Unsure of whether he had three or six months left to live, he spent his final moments seeking to make restitution for his many acts; among other things, he apologized to Dukakis.

"Beginning to think," Camus writes, "is beginning to be undermined." It is difficult to imagine a better word. All our self-constructed securities crumble and give way beneath us. We precipitously fall — into what? The old, pat answers give no comfort; they no longer seem to work. Our lives are propped up with feeble justifications, rationalizations, and clichés that give way under the weight of human experience.

sound and fury

Why is mortality a problem for a truly happy life? In Jean-Paul Sartre's short story *The Wall*, three prisoners in the Spanish civil war are sentenced to be executed the following morning. Pablo, the main character, seizes the opportunity to size up his life. He remembers the goring of a young man in a running of the bulls, he summons up the faces of relatives and friends, he recalls the taste of favorite foods, he relives the pursuit of women and liberty. And he comments: "I took everything as seriously as if I were immortal." But now death promises to change everything. "At that moment I felt that I had my whole life in front of me and I thought, 'It's a damned lie.' It was worth nothing because it was finished. . . . I wanted to tell myself, this is a beautiful life. But I couldn't pass judgment on it; it was only a sketch; I had spent my time counterfeiting eternity."[2] One momentary blip on the screen of eternity; one tiny speck in the cosmos. The grave swallows up all our accomplishments. It cuts us off from all our relationships, goals, and aspirations. Death disenchants everything. In the end we are simply nothing.

Annihilation. We fill our lives with work and school, books and television, vacations and avocations, our families and friends, yet the end is always the same — in the end we all die and are nothing, forever. In the end we are all, as the Eastern sages write, food for worms. Some of us are fatter than others, but all of us are worm food.

My young students, brimming with immortality, often wonder why Sartre and Camus get so worked up about the finality of death. Death is, after all, so far off and you won't be around to miss your relationships or care if no one marks your passing. But suppose, I ask them, you knew that you were going to lapse into an irreversible coma. How would you feel? You would be alive but not conscious — cut off from the outside world; severed from your job, relationships, and prospects. All of your life goals would be unattainable. The seconds race into minutes, which speed into hours; you are propelled into that final moment when you are transformed from an active, independent member of the human race to a dependent vegetable. How would you feel? We will not all lapse into a coma, but we will all die.

Feel the pressure of mortality. It is diametrically opposed to our passion for living — and it, not our passion for life, will win out.

2. Jean-Paul Sartre, *The Wall (Intimacy) and Other Stories,* trans. Lloyd Alexander (New York: Peter Nevill, 1950), 11.

> Tomorrow, and tomorrow, and tomorrow,
> Creeps in this petty pace from day to day,
> To the last syllable of recorded time;
> And all our yesterdays have lighted fools
> The way to dusty death. Out, out, brief candle!
> Life's but a walking shadow, a poor player,
> That struts and frets his hour upon the stage,
> And then is heard no more. It is a tale
> Told by an idiot, full of sound and fury,
> Signifying nothing.
>
> *Macbeth* 5.5.19-28

I have always found it sobering to attend funerals and then see how quickly life goes on with scarcely any notice of the recently deceased. We die, and the world of bicycle racing and barn dancing and diaper changing goes right on. We believe we are indispensable, but the attitude of people upon our death belies such wishful thinking. Their thoughts quickly return to their jobs, families, friends, and other diversions — perhaps commenting, "Life must go on. Life is, after all, for the living."

the sleep of life

Samuel Beckett's *Waiting for Godot* depicts life in a purposeless, pointless universe where people bide their time in habits and boredom until their inevitable death. Waiting interminably for Godot — an informing vision, perhaps God, that can give a point to their pointless lives — the main characters talk nonsense and perform nonsensical tasks in an attempt to ignore their hopeless situation. Their occasionally lucid patter presents Beckett's grim view of the world. Obsessed by time, which hastily and incessantly marks their progression toward the grave and nothingness, Pozzo exclaims:

115

Have you not done tormenting me with your accursed time? It's abominable. When! When! One day, is that not enough for you, one day he went dumb, one day I went blind, one day we'll go deaf, one day we were born, one day we'll die, the same day, the same second, is that not enough for you? They give birth astride of a grave, the light gleams an instant, then it's night once more.[3]

If we deeply desire earthly significance and recognize how infinitely unlikely we are to attain it, how do we go on living? Camus writes of "the sleep necessary to life." We fashion a comfortable routine that blinds us to our hopelessly limited position in the universe and time. We live automatically and uncritically, scarcely pausing to reflect on our lives. Society imposes a set of trivial customs on us, which we dutifully and contentedly follow, thereby gaining a false sense of security. Keeping our noses to the grindstone, however, we ignore both our greatest possibilities and our inevitable destiny. We rise early on Monday and work at jobs that most of us find unsatisfying and return home for supper, television, and bed. Tuesday we rise early and go to work and return home for supper, television, and bed. Wednesday — work and sex. Thursday — work and bowling. Friday — work and a beer. Saturday — mow the lawn. Sunday — church, popcorn, and a movie. Own two cars, have an attractive spouse and obedient children, vacation two weeks a year. Life can be an endless, repetitive sequence of hours, days, and years: Monday, Tuesday, Wednesday, Thursday, Friday, Saturday, Sunday, January, February, March, 1996, 1997, 1998. Habit is the sleep necessary to life. Habit, the message of *Godot*, is a great deadener.

3. Samuel Beckett, *Waiting for Godot* (New York: Grove Weidenfeld, 1954), 58.

the dream

We want our lives to be an adventure, not a dull routine. We don't want to live the life of meaningless automation. For our lives to be an adventure and not merely a disconnected series of discrete and perhaps occasionally exciting activities, there must be a worthy ending. But is there?

I had a dream last night. I entered into a world in which I thought that I was the only person who existed. This world consisted almost entirely of huge waves of silky white cloth, layer upon smoky layer, through which my body traveled by osmosis. Surrounded by the billowy, warm sheets, I felt an overwhelming urge to move — to burrow through this vast whiteness. But to where? I had no goal and no purpose. I couldn't see where my journeys might take me — it was the same snowy whiteness in every direction. But I felt compelled to move and even took pleasure in it; I was proud of my speed and the vast distances that I traveled. The sense of my body moving against the soft silk was exhilarating. Yet, in the brief moments when I stopped for rest, I was plagued with the questions "Where am I going?" and "Why?" In spite of my temporary anxieties, I plunged on through my milky textile sea.

My sensation of invigoration gave way to an overwhelming sense of loneliness as I came to believe that only I existed in this world. I felt a deep longing for other persons. My desire was shortly satisfied as I soon bumped into another person. Intent on establishing our burrowing prowess, our speed, and flushed with our own sense of accomplishment, we quickly began to resent each other and the threat that each presented to the other's sense of supremacy. Although both of us were lonely, we quickly returned to our private journeys.

I take this dream as a metaphor for the human condition: On our own we are moving, but with no ultimate goal. We are actors with no director. We take pride in our accomplishments, which temporarily give us a sense of meaning and purpose, but in brief moments of respite we feel insignificant, anxious, and lonely. We set out on our quest for significance at the expense of other people. We need others to recognize our name and to value us. So our need for significant human contact is doomed to frustration. We are lonely egos, briefly tranquilized by custom and character, darting about without purpose until we die and are forgotten.

reflection

When was the last time you took a walk in the woods, alone? How long has it been since you drove your car without the radio playing or were at home without the television or stereo turned on? When did you last sit by yourself in a quiet room and honestly reflect on your life? When did you last see a movie or read a book that did more than entertain you, that caused you to question your values or even your life? When did you not repress those feelings which, if entertained, might undermine?

This section of the book is an attempt to consider how faith in God gives our lives meaning. It is an attempt to make us all stop and think; to think, remember Camus, is to begin to be undermined. If we honestly face our mortality, our temporality, our insignificance, we will surely feel undermined. But we tear down only to see how faith can build us up. How does faith — authentic faith — help us honestly face our doubts, guilt, and even death? In the following chapters, I explore some of our attempts to find meaning and happiness and show how they lead to despair and brokenness. The central theme is the attempt to create a self of abiding value. We are creatures, not creators, so our attempts to create a self are doomed. Our true self and happiness are found through faith in God.

Let me briefly outline the plan of the second portion of the book. In Chapter 8, I set the stage for exploring faith by looking at how we attempt to create a self independent of God — without faith. Our life projects involve the construction of a magnificent, solid, enduring self. This self, I shall argue, is constructed on the flimsy foundation of the adulation and memory of others. This foundation will crumble as will the self built upon it. Without faith, our self is rooted in futility and despair.

Chapter 9 focuses on the way that faith helps us to reject our created self and to accept our authentic self before God. For Kierkegaard the first step toward becoming an authentic person is to look at oneself honestly, unsupported by the deceitful props of our character and roles. The only way to become a genuine self is to transcend the deceptive self. Only at this point can one truly relate to God and become an authentic human being. Only by giving up the merely cultural, personal, finite, and perishing values may one relate, in faith, to the Source of infinite value.

Chapter 10 could bear the label, "Warning: This Chapter Contains Philosophically Explicit Material!" This chapter is written in a more academic style and lays the philosophical foundation of the second portion of the book. I present Kierkegaard's stages on life's way as means for understanding the quest for happiness. He powerfully and creatively exposes the follies of the various stages of life. The only way to live a genuinely meaningful life is to leap into the religious stage where one discovers forgiveness and freedom.

In the final chapter I discuss our deepest human needs — for security and peace, for assurance that the world is not hostile to our plans and prospects, for the belief that our journey has a goal. These needs are satisfied, I shall argue, only through faith in God. There is also a need to redeem time: we want to seize the time, to fill it with meaningful and worthy activities, but we have squandered precious time, and it is in increasingly short supply. We cannot get time back, but can time be redeemed? I conclude the book with a challenge to accept the adventure of life, to be, as Eliot writes, "still and still moving."

In this section of the book I attempt to make good on the claim

I made in the introduction: the benefits of faith are so great that, in spite of life's darkness, faith ought to be pursued. Even if we cannot resolve all of our doubts, we need to be coaxed into caring that the quest for faith is worth the effort. Finding our authentic self makes the endeavor worthwhile.

chapter 8

What's in a Name?

It has never been easy for me to understand the obliteration of time, to accept, as others seem to do, the swelling and corresponding shrinkage of seasons or the conscious acceptance that one year has ended and another begun. There is something here that speaks of our essential helplessness and how the greater substance of our lives is bound up with waste and opacity. Even the sentence parts seize on the tongue, so that to say "Twelve years passed" is to deny the fact of biographical logic. How can so much time hold so little, how can it be taken from us? Months, weeks, days, hours misplaced — and the most precious time of life, too, when our bodies are at their greatest strength, and open, as they never will be again, to the onslaught of sensation. For twelve years, from age fourteen to twenty-six, my father, young Cuyler Goodwill, rose early, ate a bowl of oatmeal porridge, walked across the road to the quarry where he worked a nine-and-a-half hour day, then returned to the chill and meagerness of his parents' house and prepared for an early bed.

The recounting of a life is a cheat, of course; I admit the truth of this; even our own stories are obscenely distorted; it is a wonder really that we keep faith with the simple container of our existence.

Carol Shields, *The Stone Diaries*

ooooo

recounting a life

What comes to mind when you reminisce about your grandparents? Do you know where they grew up; what they did for a living; whether and where they went to church; what kinds of books, if any, they read; how they passed their leisure time; how they voted in national elections; whether they lived their dreams and were satisfied with their lot; what kind of parents they were? When your parents recount the lives of their parents, what stands out? Their courage, triumph over poverty, good looks, piety, parental care? Did they make a mark or money in their careers, perhaps authoring a book, earning a fortune, or penning a song? If you were to walk down the streets of the town where they lived, would people still remember them and speak fondly of them? Is that town or the world any different, any better, because they lived there once?

I have vivid memories of my own grandmother, Anna Catherine Leech. Grandma was good, steadfast, and decent. Her life was unassuming, ordinary, but in her life there was splendor in the ordinary. She was a single mother long before Murphy Brown made it fashionable. It was not a lifestyle choice for her; her husband died young. It took determination and perseverance to raise five children alone. And she took pride in the accomplishments of her children and grandchildren, attending basketball games, track meets, concerts, and graduations for nearly a score of people over virtually three score years. She unpretentiously and with ease always did what was upright and appropriate. For her, there could be no question of doing otherwise. Virtue was strong in her nature, knit into her very bones. She was unfailingly kind and long-suffering; she was possessed of good humor; she was self-sacrificial, hard-working, and devoted to her family. The values manifested in Grandma's life are considered old-fashioned. God forbid they ever go out of fashion. As I play with my son, Evan, flesh partly of Grandma's flesh and the most recent of her descendants, I hope that these characteristics will be passed on in my family from generation to generation. I could hope for nothing better.

When Grandma died in 1994, I was asked to eulogize her at the funeral. With fear and delight I assumed the awesome responsibility

123

of recounting her life. Although my young children sat in the congregation listening attentively, I wondered, sadly, what they would remember of this extraordinary woman. What remains of her life but the memories of her children and their children?

Do you know your great-grandparents? If you can, try to remember the names of *their* parents. Just the names. Perhaps you are fortunate enough to remember this far back. Now try to recall the name of *their* parents. In just a few generations, our ancestors have been forgotten even by those most likely to remember; *we can't even remember their names.* How likely is it that your descendants, or anyone else, will remember your name after you die? Just your name. Our most precious deeds, our singular acts of heroism, our noble aspirations, and our determined legacy vanish long before our name is last spoken on the lips of our not-so-distant descendants.

The half-life of our memories is desperately brief. We are slapped into life with a scream and ushered out in a box and a whimper. The grandest reminiscence reduces an entire life to a few, feeble words that vanish on each recounting. An entire life in five hundred minuscule words, now my granddaughter's three hundred words, now my great-grandson's one hundred words, now my great-great-grandchildren's silence. We die once, Boethius writes, when we lose our life, but we die a second time when our memory is finally obliterated:

Where now are the bones of good Fabricius?
What is Brutus now, or stern old Cato?
What little fame is left them — just their names
In a few old stories!
And if we read and learn their glorious names
Do we then know the dead?
And so you too will all be quite forgotten,
Nor can fame make you known by any man.
And if you think you may live longer yet

At least as a name alive on the lips of men,
When your last day takes even this from you,
There's still to come
That second death.[1]

Napoleon was fond of reminding his generals that the churchyards are full of people who thought they were indispensable.

making a name for ourselves

The desire to make a name for ourselves infuses everything we do. We long to be remembered, to do something supremely important or significant, and to feel that our lives are special, unique. We do not want to be forgotten; we do not want our lives to be trivial. Our quest for significance is a prime motivator behind our actions. We want to make a name for ourselves.

I remember sitting on the stage at my high school graduation and feeling very special among the small group of students who had graduated in the top ten. There, in the balcony, were the general run-of-the-mill students. But up here, on the stage, we were different, even special; we stood out, and everyone was there looking at us, and we were pleased. When the inspirational but eminently forgettable graduation speaker noted that the world eagerly awaited us for its transformation, we, on the stage, knew that the world didn't have long to wait.

My academic successes continued into college, and I graduated with high honors with a double major in Philosophy and Religious Studies. I was destined for greater things, and when other people acknowledged as much, I was delighted.

1. Boethius, *The Consolation of Philosophy*, trans. V. E. Watts (New York: Penguin, 1969), 75.

Then came graduate school. I was shocked at how smart all of the other students seemed and began to wonder if the department had made a mistake in admitting me. But I found my way, developed some confidence, and proceeded to complete my degree. As I neared graduation, I compared myself to my brilliant professors, into whose ranks I would shortly enter. It became my hope that I would at least be mediocre, perhaps even a little above average. All my life I believed myself on top and arrogantly delighted in it. Now, for the first time in my life, my goal was mediocrity. I hoped to find my place somewhere near the middle of a half-million university professors.

I was all promise in high school and college, but by the time I graduated with my doctorate there was no fulfillment. I had a common reaction to completing a dissertation: depression. I had worked two and a half years to produce a manuscript of some two hundred pages on an obscure topic that was typed, bound, read by four professors, and placed on the stacks in the library to gather dust. I was about to enter a world of extremely gifted people where, I feared, my intellectual inadequacies would be unmasked and I would be doomed to failure at ever making a name for myself in my chosen profession. My self-esteem dove with my growing realization of the difficulty of making my mark.

We all need to stand out, but this becomes increasingly difficult as we move from smaller, less demanding groups to larger, more competitive ones. The great high school football player goes to a large university and sits on the bench for four years. The honors student finds when she gets to college that her high school teachers were easy graders. The best accounting student at the state college gets a job in a firm in New York City and realizes he is a small fish in a big pond. The real world is full of talented people, and it is the rare person who stands out. Even those who do stand out eventually get swallowed up in the vastness of space and time upon entering the biggest group for comparison: the world at large throughout human history. In *The Consolation of Philosophy*, Boethius reminds us of how puny we are when seeking significance or glory within this vast world:

You have learned from astronomical proofs that the whole circle of our earth is but a point in comparison with the extent of the whole heavens; that is, if it is compared in size with the celestial sphere, it is judged to have no size at all. Of this very tiny part of the universe only a quarter . . . is inhabited by living things known to us. If in your imagination you subtract from that quarter all that is covered by seas and marshes and all the regions which extend in dried-up deserts, only a very narrow portion indeed is left for habitation by men. Now is it in this tightly-enclosed and tiny point, itself but part of a point, that you think of spreading your reputation, of glorifying your name? What grandeur or magnificence can glory have, contracted within such small and narrow limits? Consider . . . that in this little habitable enclosure there live many nations, different in language and customs and in their whole ways of life; because of the difficulties of travel, and differences of language, . . . the fame not merely of individual men but even of cities cannot reach them all. . . . Do you then see how narrow, how contracted is that glory which you labor to increase and spread abroad?[2]

At some point or other in our lives, we will all feel tiny and insignificant, anonymous and ignored. Most of our hearts will tell us that we feel small but need to feel large, feel insignificant but want to be significant, feel ignored but desire recognition. We may lower our aspirations to accommodate our limitations, but our desire to stand out cannot be diminished.

I made the mistake of asking one of my students about her part in the school play in front of the class. She replied that she was a cat and that her only "speaking" part was a single meow. We laughed together about her role, but I sensed her embarrassment when she expressed the desire for at least one line in the play — just a brief dramatic entrance with a line she could deliver with pomp and power — to let us all know

2. Boethius, *Consolation of Philosophy,* 73.

127

that she was there. How often in life we have had the same desire: to have that one line and deliver it well.

We dream of being Michael Jordan, Mel Gibson, or Madonna. We watch action movies and long to be the hero. We read a powerful book and think, "I wish I had written that." Someone makes a clever remark that we wish we had. Our dreams tell us what our intellects deny — we want our lives to be recognized as supremely important.

In an early scene of the film *Amadeus,* a priest comes to hear the confession of Antonio Salieri, a very old man who has just attempted suicide and who alleges that, years ago, he killed Mozart. Salieri, at one time the most famous composer in Europe, plays a small piece of his own music on the piano for the priest.

"You must know this," Salieri says.

"I can't say that I do," the priest confesses.

"Here, how about this?"

"I regret it is not too familiar."

"Here, what about this one?" Finally Salieri plays a piece that causes the priest, with great relief, to smile, nod in recognition, and hum along.

"Yes, I know that!" the priest says. "Oh, that's charming! I'm sorry, I didn't know you wrote that."

"I didn't. That was Mozart."

"Do you know who I am?" Salieri had asked at the beginning of the interview. "That makes no difference," the priest had replied. "All are equal in God's eyes." But to Salieri it made all the difference in the world. As a youth, he had prayed to God: "Lord, make me a great composer. Let me celebrate your glory through music and be celebrated myself. Make me famous through the world, dear God. Make me immortal. After I die, let people speak my name forever with love for what I wrote. In return, I will give you my chastity, my industry, my deepest humility, every hour of my life." Over time, though, Salieri's music has come to be eclipsed by Mozart's; he has been robbed of any opportunity for musical immortality. "I am extinct," he says to the priest. "My music is growing fainter, all the time fainter." He is being forgotten well before his death; he has lived just long enough to witness, in Boethius's haunting terms, his second death.

In midlife, Leo Tolstoy was plagued by his impending death and contemplated the prospect that he and his works would soon be forgotten: "If not today, then tomorrow sickness and death will come (indeed, they were already approaching) to everyone, to me, and nothing will remain except stench and worms. My deeds, whatever they may be, will be forgotten sooner or later, and I myself will be no more."[3] That Tolstoy's work would not be remembered trivialized it in his own eyes and disenchanted his desire for human activity. Why work when my greatest accomplishments will shortly be forgotten?

We fill our selves with the richest and most sustaining food available to us — fame, fortune, family, friendship — but one day we will be trundled into a box, lowered into the ground, forgotten by friends and family, and finally devoured by worms. Worm food, that's our destiny. "You die and then you rot," said a famous rotting philosopher.

The insignificance we feel as part of the larger world explains in part our need to belong to small communities where we can feel esteemed. We join a church, or a civic organization, a bridge club, a knitting group, a book discussion. *Cheers,* the famous bar of the television show, was a place "where everybody knows your name." In each group we strive to make our mark. We walk away from our Tuesday night bowling club full of pride because we finished first. We feel good about the book discussion because it gives us a chance to display our wisdom and have it affirmed. We don't play bridge to lose. Our self-esteem expands if we are demonstrably better mothers, knitters, volunteers, or members of the church. Even the holiest, or most moral, of ventures can be a feeding ground for our insatiable egos.

I don't wish to impugn our participation in such groups; we need

3. Leo Tolstoy, *Confession,* trans. David Patterson (New York: Norton, 1983), 30.

them to live. But the motivation behind our participation needs to be unmasked. We seek significance on a grand scale but are frustrated in our attempts to attain it. So we divert our quest for significance to a smaller scale and try to content ourselves with that. And it often works, until we recognize — when we lose our job, when we get to age forty-five and feel we have really accomplished nothing, when our marriage begins to fail, or when we are passed over for a promotion — that we have never ceased striving for glory on the grander scale at all.

what's in a name?

As so many expectant couples do, my wife and I compiled separate lists of potential names before each of our children were born. We went through each other's list, crossing out names that were not acceptable. When we were done, we shared our lists and had to justify the elimination of certain names. Some names seemed, to one or the other of us, too sissy for a boy or too masculine for a girl. Some names seemed old-fashioned, nerdy, or highfalutin. Many otherwise perfectly acceptable names were eliminated because of their associations with people we knew back in childhood. This name conjured up images of "tubby," that one of "bully," and others evoked various images: "hippie," "druggie," "lazy," "gossipy," "snob." The association of name and character ruined the name for one or the other of us. Fortunately, we managed to scrape up one or two positive associations and were able, in good conscience, to name our children!

It is not uncommon in naming a child to pick a familial name, with all the strengths of the parent or grandparent or family. Or to select a name that connects the person named to their ethnic heritage. Or to choose the name of a revered biblical or historical figure. The surname becomes the legacy passed on from generation to generation,

130

the collective strength of an entire clan. No male heirs and one fears that the name will be lost.

Names are not mere interchangeable tags pinned to people for ease of identification; *names are shorthand representations of the essence of a person.* Ronald Reagan, Saddam Hussein, Gandhi, Bill Gates, Michael Jordan, Pope John Paul II. Each of these individuals is a repository of attributes summoned at the mere mention of their names. Their names can elicit revulsion or attraction, tedium or excitement, anger or delight, somber reflection or easy disdain. A meaningless conjunction of symbols cannot have that effect; the name stands for the set of properties we attribute to the person. The naming of a person we know includes a judgment of that person's character and worth. In addition, there is always a sizing up; when we name someone, we peek into a person's soul.

When people who know you or have heard of you speak your name, your personality and character come to mind. *Making a name for ourselves is our attempt to influence the judgments people make when hearing or uttering our name.* Through sheer force of effort or accomplishment, we hope to erect a self that cannot be diminished by those who know our name; when the sizing up is done we want to insure that we have been sized up properly and that we have instilled our worth in the mind of the other person.

The use of descriptive nicknames is an attempt on our part to influence the attribution of positive traits to ourselves. Others, of course, may provide us with a nickname — flattering or otherwise — that they think captures our essence. If we allow its continued use, we are forcing others to ascribe certain properties to us. Nicknames aid in the making of a first impression where people initially and on the basis of extremely limited information begin to latch on to our essence and to make judgments about us. Even without a nickname, our names can often trigger negative associations in people who don't even know us ("Another Mike. Great. He's probably like that obnoxious Mike I had to work with in my last job").

131

We are constantly sizing up, judging, narrowing down the world, fitting it and ourselves into manageable categories by naming things. And we are likewise being managed when people name or classify us. Naming gives us power over another person or group of persons because we can limit our associations with the name to those that elevate ourselves. Entire groups of people can be dismissed from the competition of life by naming them "commie" or "liberal." When we call someone a "commie," for instance, we diminish them, push them to the periphery of concern, and thereby shrink the class of people who count. In so doing, we expand our own self-worth.

If someone is peering into our soul, we don't want them to see us in all our nakedness and shame. We want them to speak our name with respect and recognition of our stature. We want our name magnified by our genuine accomplishments, not trivialized by our shortcomings. In wanting to make a name for ourselves, we want to make ourselves known. We want to stand out. We want to create our essence so solidly and so profoundly that it cannot be discounted by those who think or use our name.

In the powerful play *The Death of a Salesman,* Willie Loman, a lifelong traveling salesman, is desperately and pathetically anonymous. Ignored by family and friends, he claims that he is vital in New England and challenges his detractors to go to Filene's, go to the hub in Boston and call out the name Willie Loman. His name, he claims, is known in New England. His wish is to die the death of a salesman — hundreds of people, who recognize his vitality, will attend his funeral. In the climax of the play, Willie's estranged son declares: "I am a dime a dozen and so are you." Enraged, his exaggerated self-worth attacked, Willie screams: "I am not a dime a dozen; I am Willie Loman." He is right: he is Willie Loman — Willie Low Man. His nature is captured in his name. His wife realizes that he needs people to pay attention, needs to feel that his work and life matter. But when Willie dies, no one attends his funeral except a few obligatory relatives.

life is a race

Thomas Hobbes, the great political theorist, remarked that "Life is a race with no other good but to be foremost." Our thirst for glory was one of the foundations upon which Hobbes built his political theory: without the constraints imposed by government we would stop at nothing, even the taking of human life, on the path to self-glorification. He writes of our deep need for glory: "For every man looketh that his companions should value him, at the same rate he sets upon himself: and upon all signs of contempt, or undervaluing, naturally endeavours, as far as he dares . . . to extort a greater value from his contemners, by damage."[4] We are far too civil to inflict damage by clubs, knives, or bullets; and were we to attempt to fulfill the desire to do so, we would be restrained by our government; but is there, underneath this thin veneer of civility, an unacknowledged fear of punishment disguising the desire to win the competition of life at all costs? How do defanged and declawed — that is, civilized — people inflict damage on those competing against them in the race for honor and fame?

Our self-worth is constituted comparatively — by dividing the world up in ways that ascribe ultimate significance to ourselves. We diminish the world to expand our selves. We start by dividing the world in half according to sex — preferring our own sex to that of the other — "I'm glad that I was born a man (woman). . . ." Entire cultures eliminate female contenders from the race for glory by preventing their participation in the workforce, civic life, the arts and sciences, and even the marketplace. That infant girls can be regularly discarded at birth in some cultures indicates the immediate lack of value attributed to them. Eliminating more than fifty percent of the contestants from the competition means the race is half won.

We also believe that our cultural heritage is intrinsically prefer-

---

4. Thomas Hobbes, *Leviathan* (New York: Dutton, 1924), 64.

133

able to others — not simply different but better, in a moral and even spiritual sense. American ethnocentrism is appealing because it accords us a status above peoples of other cultures. "I'm proud to be an American" is often more than an innocent, patriotic slogan; it can involve demoting people of other nationalities to secondary status. The terms we use to describe other cultures are heavily value-laden and tilt the scales in favor of our own culture. We call other races and cultures "backward," "primitive," "savage," "pagan," "uncivilized," "third-world." Those skilled in the process of sociolinguistic derision can eliminate virtually every other culture from the race for glory.

Our racist epithets relegate entire classes of people in our own society to secondary status — niggers, honkies, hymies, wops, chinks, dagos, spics. Of course, we are too civilized, too politically correct, to utter these slurs ourselves; we leave that to the "less enlightened" among us and content ourselves with racist attitudes. Racial and ethnic prejudice instantly elevates us above entire classes of people.

We further justify our position within our own society by demarcating the social strata. We believe that it is preferable to be middle-class than to be among the filthy rich or among those tacky rich people who love to display their "new money." Rich people notoriously put up their noses at poor people. "Let them eat cake." Poor people have no monopoly on virtue, yet they can also believe themselves to be morally superior to both the rich and middle classes. Why even God esteems the poor above the rest: "Blessed are ye poor." Who can resist the divine seal of approval on one's state and the corresponding condemnation of all those not included? Poverty and fortune alike are worn as badges of honor. Regardless of our station, we are tempted to think that it is morally superior to any other.

We often take the schools that we attend as evidence of our worth. If we have been denied admission to Harvard, we rationalize — "They put too much emphasis on test scores." Or conversely, we feel the need to justify our existence by touting where we did go to school:

"Did you see the latest rankings of colleges in *U.S. News & World Report?* My alma mater was rated in the top ten." "We may not have any world-renowned scholars teaching here at my small college, but I hear that at Stanford graduate students do all the teaching."

We come up with similar rationalizations if we are passed over for a job or, worse, fired. Instead of taking these rejections as reflections of our own character, we blame the employer. We tell ourselves that they weren't hiring in good faith or that they preferred women and minorities or that the boss couldn't handle an employee who was more talented than the employer. The weight of losing one's job and believing oneself to be deficient often leads to a dramatic loss of self-esteem and deep depression. We require rationalizations to maintain our mental health.

We develop elaborate social defense mechanisms to keep ourselves from feeling anonymous and mediocre. We employ various strategies to convince ourselves that we are better workers, students, golfers, parents, spouses, and people than those around us. Or we give up on our private quest for glory and invest all our energies vaunting the accomplishments of our children. Would we push our children so hard if we were prevented from bragging about them?

We are often unhappy when others are rewarded or honored and we are not. We cannot let ourselves lose the race, so if others are successful we rush to diminish their success ("She's beautiful, drives a Porsche and lives in a mansion, but she isn't *really* happy"). We must be the winner in this competition, even if only in our own minds. What is gossip but a devious strategy of self-elevation at the expense of another? If we can pass on that the beautiful owner of the mansion is an alcoholic whose third marriage has failed, we have succeeded in diminishing them and elevating ourselves. We are often secretly pleased when we learn of the misfortune of others.

One telling psychological clue to how competitive our lives are is the difference in how we explain failures in ourselves and others. When we show up late for a meeting, it isn't our fault: the car wouldn't start, traffic was heavy, or the kids were sick. When another person shows up late, they are to blame: they are irresponsible, unorganized, uncaring. Since we all regularly fail to fulfill our duties, there is ample opportunity for us to portray ourselves to ourselves in a favorable light and to paint others in an unfavorable light.

Our self-identity is determined comparatively — "At least I'm not as dumb as Ralph"; "I'm more well-rounded than Gillian." "Aren't our children more handsome than the Jones's?" We size someone up in a phrase or a look that cuts them down to size. We are the Pharisee looking down on the Publican: "Thank God, I'm not like other people. I pray, I fast, I tithe." We suck the value out of those we deem beneath us and draw it into our incessantly demanding self.

Our need to feel superior runs deep. To do so we tell ourselves stories that ascribe to us self-worth at the expense of others. Our lives are filled with conventions, both calculated and unthinking, to please others, to get ahead, to gain power, to be recognized, to stand out. We are social creatures who need others to munch on to feed our starving egos.

Our efforts to gain glory, honor, and fame are doomed by the vastness of the cosmos. Our finest efforts are swallowed up in space and time. We must believe that we are winning the race of life, but we are doomed from the outset.

chapter 9

Searching for My Self

Now the dread of possibility holds him as its prey, until it can deliver him saved into the hands of faith. In no other place does he find repose . . . he who went through the curriculum of misfortune offered by possibility lost everything, absolutely everything, in a way that no one has lost it in reality. If in this situation he did not behave falsely towards possibility, if he did not attempt to talk around the dread which would save him, then he received everything back again, as in reality no one ever did even if he received everything tenfold, for the pupil of possibility receives infinity.

Ernest Becker, *The Denial of Death*

Whatever faith may be, and whatever answers it may give, and to whomsoever it gives them, every such answer gives to the finite existence of man an infinite meaning, a meaning not destroyed by sufferings, deprivations, or death.

Tolstoy, *My Confession*

Do not let me hear
Of the wisdom of old men, but rather of their folly,
Their fear of fear and frenzy, their fear of possession,
Of belonging to another, or to others, or to God.
The only wisdom we can hope to acquire
Is the wisdom of humility: humility is endless.

T. S. Eliot, *Four Quartets*

ooooo

In the previous chapter I argued that our sense of self is derived comparatively, typically at the expense of others. We diminish others in order to magnify ourselves. Self-esteem is granted, curiously, by the other; we need the other to recognize, value, even esteem our selves. All of this we cannot give to our self. Our cleverest conceits to gain glory at the expense of the other run counter to our need for the other to value us. Who among us would value the other in full knowledge that the other is likewise seeking glory at our expense? It is folly to admire the person who plucks merit from your soul through gossip, slander, prejudice, and contempt. Our futile attempts at self-justification require, yet disdain, the other.

Like animals, human beings require food and shelter for their survival; unlike animals, however, humans also feed on self-esteem. The results of diminished self-worth are depression, alcoholism, drug abuse, loneliness, neuroses and psychoses, and even suicide. We cannot live without self-esteem, yet our attempts to gain it are, when considered carefully and honestly, bound for despair. No one truly aware of the human condition — that we feed on others to bolster our own self-esteem — can be pleased with the insipid, begrudging honor he receives. The prospect of crossing the finish line first begins to look less likely when we realize that in the race for self-esteem, the vast majority of those running this race are losers, and our fellow competitors are chiefly interested in winning at any cost and will do all they can to trip up whomever they must. The so-called adulation of others is emptied of its power to bestow self-esteem when we perceive that it conceals secret and not-so-secret scorn.

If, in the race of life, you are so proficient that I can't trip you up, I can still hope that you will trip yourself up or that someone else will or that you will drop out of the race altogether. Death removes many worthy competitors from the field, but life is prolific, and younger, worthier opponents keep entering the race. We may do our best to narrow the field and come out on top, but others are doing the same. It's a race we cannot win.

139

Pinning our hopes on immortality is likewise folly. The desire for eternal fame is undone by physical death and the death of memories of us. The self that persists in the memories of others is a slender reed trampled in that final remembrance. Except for the most outstanding and heroic, numbering precious few, our legacy, like our lives, endures but a moment. Our lives flare up like a match, burn briefly bright, and are quickly snuffed out.

Our life projects involve the construction of a magnificent, solid, and enduring self constructed on the flimsy foundation of the adulation and memory of others. The foundation will crumble and so will the self built upon it. No one can grasp this truth about their self and avoid anxiety or disappointment. Genuine self-knowledge leads us to the brink of despair.

In this chapter I will examine Ernest Becker's perceptive analysis of the human condition in his book *The Denial of Death*.[1] The observations of the previous chapters have been exceedingly grim; the prospects for a genuinely meaningful life are desperately thin. The human condition is grave, and so far we have little grounds to hope for freedom from worry and hopelessness. I believe there is reason to hope, and we shall seek it, as Becker does, in the writings of Søren Kierkegaard. Here is the ground of hope for Kierkegaard: The constructed self must die so that the real self can come to life through faith in God. The self that we have created and coddled is a snare and a delusion, necessary surely for facing the uncertainties of life and the certainty of death, but one that must die for us to live without anxiety and despair. It is only in dying to our constructed self that we can find our true self.

1. Ernest Becker, *The Denial of Death* (New York: Free Press, 1973).

creating a self

In order to understand how we develop our sense of self, we need to delve a bit into developmental psychology. Since I have no expertise in this area, all errors must be attributed to Becker! I am raising three children and was once a child myself, so I have experience without expertise. Having thus declared my ignorance, I shall now proceed.

Infants are ejected from their warm, safe, connected, and soothing environment into a cold, dangerous, separated, and perturbing one. The child's sense of self, or ego, develops in response to this new, exciting, and terrifying environment. The world is a terrifying place, and the infant perceives it so. Given the choice (and a modicum of intelligence and the ability to choose), no right-minded infant would fail to plunge back into the familiar, serene, munificent womb. That infants prefer the womb to their extra-womb existence is evident in the satisfaction they find in conditions that recreate the womb, such as listening to recordings of womb sounds and sleeping in the fetal position with the pressure of the crib or a blanket against their heads.

Although infants are not self-conscious, their sense of self develops nonetheless in response to their new environment. If they are treated with suitable care and love — fed when hungry, changed when wet and soiled, allowed to sleep when weary, held regularly and often, especially when overstimulated — they will begin to see themselves at the center of the universe. During the initial months, they don't distinguish themselves from their surroundings — they are all in all. When they begin to differentiate themselves from others and from objects, however, they continue to sense that the world revolves around them. They sense this because, as far as they can tell, the world does indeed revolve around them. To maturing infants, the world is a tiny place that they dominate, populated by a small number of people, all of whom grant them virtually unlimited attention and care.

As they grow in consciousness and self-consciousness, they per-

141

ceive more and allow more bits of reality into their purview. If they are overstimulated or if their needs are not satisfied, they will cry and then sleep. These two activities cut them off from the overwhelming stimuli around them. As they grow older, their crying and sleeping defenses diminish and they require new coping mechanisms for closing off the blooming and buzzing confusion confronting them. Their eyes allow them to focus on and, hence, experience more. Their arms and legs carry them to new and distant places. These new experiences require categories for understanding, managing, and limiting the world.

If infants have been parented properly and sheltered from life's dangers, they will feel loved and secure. When my first son, Will, was born, I jokingly pointed his face toward the window to look out onto a cold, gloomy January day in New England. "It's a cold, cruel world out there, Will," I told him. "Better get used to it." And then I held him close and passed him to his mother when he began to cry. "It's all right," we told him. We kissed his soft head while the world, saturated with viruses, diseases, automobiles, serial killers, and death, conspired against him. We all know that it is *not* all right and that there is a great deal to fear and that infants, unprotected by their parents, are the most vulnerable. Their secure sense of self develops a safe distance from the truth.

Infants absorb the twin untruths that the world is safe and that it revolves around them. If infants and toddlers were not nurtured on these two untruths, though, they would grow insecure and anxious and become future candidates for psychosis or neurosis. Parents have to convey these untruths to their infants to ensure their psychological health. The ego of infants is simply too fragile and would be crushed if confronted in a deep and sustained way with the truth that the world is not safe and does not revolve around them. These untruths are necessary for the creation of a solid, substantial self, one that enables maturing children to withstand the vast and indifferent universe.

142

The child's incipient narcissism is fed through the constant attention of the parent. The child doesn't require training in narcissism; it is innately present. But the child's narcissism is encouraged, refined, and developed with each feeding and caress. That the world *is* at the child's beck and call is clear; that the world *ought* to be at the child's beck and call is manifest in each incessant and demanding wail. Narcissism is encouraged and, hence, flourishes. That the child is number one in the universe seems, to the child, abundantly clear.

The birth of a sibling is a threat to the child's status as number one. Sibling rivalry is a manifestation of that underlying narcissism — the other child must be demoted in order to ensure that I remain number one. Every perceived slight or favoritism, however small, is a threat to the child's supreme place in both the family and the world. Apparently innocent phrases such as "His piece is bigger than mine!" and "You always let her stay up later!" reveal the threat posed by the other child. There is only room for one at the top.

Freud recognized that one of the primary purposes of the ego is to enable human beings to avoid anxiety.[2] It delays responses and prevents us from directly reacting to stimuli. To do so, it must label the stimuli as something "out there," differentiated from the self, not me. In delaying a response to stimuli, individuals use their wits to select an adequate rejoinder to external conditions. The ego sets up protective boundaries behind which the mind has the luxury of time to consider appropriate responses.

The ego's defense mechanism tames the world by naming it and dividing it up into categories of good, bad, and neutral. The self finds its place at the center around which the world revolves in an orderly pattern partly created by one's self (not consciously, of course, and typically through the medium of parents). In the center is the "I," no

---

2. In the next two paragraphs I follow the discussion of Ernest Becker, *The Birth and Death of Meaning: A Perspective in Psychiatry and Anthropology* (New York: Free Press, 1962).

indiscriminate ghost in the machine, but a real, substantial, enduring self. It is not one's self alone that creates the categories and names that order the world. One's sociolinguistic upbringing, for example, as directed by one's parents, slowly assists in bringing order to the chaos of experience. The toddler gradually gains control over the world by differentiation and by linguistic proficiency. Praise and blame — "Good boy!" "Naughty girl!" — help establish both safe and dangerous zones. The ego tames the world by cutting it down to size, keeping it manageable, limiting possibility.

As children grow in self-consciousness, their experience of the world expands with frightening rapidity. They become increasingly aware that there are others in competition with them, that they alone do not and cannot receive all of their parent's attention, that people devoted to them may leave them forever, that there are places they cannot go and things they cannot do. Their hands and bottoms get slapped; their cries go unanswered; their demands go unheeded. Yet they must develop mechanisms for coping, for continuing to feel supremely valued. Their character develops as a mechanism for coping with their ever-expanding reality; it must preserve their pride of place in the universe. The child's sense of self must remain large and central, while the ever-expanding universe must be circumscribed and properly situated around the self.

Parents, then, must instill in their children a sense of value that does not measure up to reality. Typically, only two people — mom and dad — believe this child to be of supreme worth. Only two people are fashioning an environment, a home, in which the child can be cherished, comforted, and nurtured; the rest of the world, people and germs included, is either indifferent or hostile. But the child must feel supremely valued even as the awareness of insignificance and of the world's vastness and indifference begins to creep into consciousness.

Becker summarizes the development of character as a necessary but dishonest response to the child's environment:

Man had to invent and create out of himself the limitations of perception and the equanimity to live on this planet. And so the core of psychodynamics, the formation of the human character, is a study in human self-limitation and in the terrifying costs of that limitation. The hostility to psychoanalysis . . . will always be a hostility against admitting that man lives by lying to himself about himself and about his world, and that character . . . is a vital lie.[3]

Human character is vital; without it we could not function in the world with equanimity. But it is a lie that masks our genuine insignificance in a vast, indifferent, and often hostile world. *Human character* — this is worth repeating — *is a vital lie.*

As the child grows older, character develops by repression as the child wishes to continue to feel significant, valued, and secure. Becker writes:

The individual has to repress globally, from the entire spectrum of his experience, if he wants to feel a warm sense of inner value and basic security. This sense of value and support is something that nature gives to each animal by the automatic instinctive programming and in the pulsating of the vital processes. But man, poor denuded creature, has to build and earn inner value and security. He must repress his smallness in the adult world, his failures to live up to adult commands and codes. He must repress his own feelings of physical and moral inadequacy, not only the inadequacy of his good intentions but also his guilt and his evil intentions. . . . And with all this, and more that we leave unsaid, he must repress the primary awesomeness of the external world.[4]

---

3. Becker, *Denial of Death*, 51.
4. Becker, *Denial of Death*, 52.

The world is too big, and we are too small, for us to walk about in full knowledge of ourselves or the world. We need our rationalizations to keep us propped up, to enable us to feel secure, to consider ourselves valued. Without the lies of character, we could not feel safe and secure.

As we leave home and move into the adult world, we assume, in even greater measure, the values, beliefs, and judgments of the wider culture. We do not so much choose these values as have them programmed into us. We come to measure our worth in terms of our socioeconomic status or by the degree to which we meet our culture's standards of beauty. The value our culture places on being slim, for example, is so powerfully, subconsciously inculcated in young girls that by the time they are self-conscious of their weight, most of them cannot possibly choose *not* to desire to be excessively slim. The same goes for gender roles, ethnic prejudices, and religious beliefs. These and countless other values and judgments, in which the child is unconsciously schooled, constitute what Becker calls a cultural hero system, "a symbolic action system, a structure of statuses and roles, customs and rules for behavior, designed to serve as a vehicle for earthly heroism."[5] The cultural hero system enables us to stand out and feel special over and against others in our ever-expanding world. As children, we are compelled to learn the techniques for standing out that adults have mastered—ambition, prejudice, competition, rationalization, elitism, nationalism, gossip, religious exclusivism, and cultural chauvinism.

Our lives are an elaborate defense mechanism designed to bolster up our self-worth. We assume roles that are fashioned to make us feel significant in spite of mounting evidence of our insignificance. The world is a vast and terrifying place, and our efforts to attain self-worth are futile; we are simply not up to the task of expanding our egos to

5. Becker, *Denial of Death*, 4.

fill the universe. Our character, while helping us to cope with reality, masks reality from us and obscures our place in the cosmos.

Our character is fundamentally dishonest, a necessary lie; without it we could not survive. If we could peel off the layers of character that allow us to feel significant in a hostile and indifferent universe and get down to our authentic, unprotected, naked self, we would feel humiliated, anxious, and even despairing.

searching for my self

The only way to live with equanimity is to perpetuate the vital lie, and we are led to wonder if it is even possible to live a genuinely meaningful life without denying the truth about our self and about our world. For Kierkegaard, the first step toward becoming an authentic person is to look at one's self honestly, unsupported by the deceitful props of character and roles. The only way to be authentic is to break through the crust of character and see into the naked heart of the beast. The only way to become a genuine self is to transcend the deceptive self and to die to one's self: "The self must be broken in order to become a self."[6]

Kierkegaard would agree that character is a vital lie. He believes that human character is a defense mechanism constructed to avoid acknowledging the "terror, perdition [and] annihilation [that] dwell next door to every man."[7] Kierkegaard, though using different terms, teaches that character is a defense mechanism against an ever expanding and terrifying reality. Most people live in a state of "shut-upness" whereby they have cut themselves off from a full perception of reality.

6. Søren Kierkegaard, *Sickness Unto Death*, trans. Walter Lowrie (Princeton: Princeton University Press, 1941), 199, quoted in Becker, *Denial of Death*, 88.

7. Søren Kierkegaard, *Concept of Dread*, trans. Walter Lowrie (Princeton: Princeton University Press, 1957), 41, quoted in Becker, *Denial of Death*, 70.

The parent's responsibility, Kierkegaard writes, is to cultivate a healthy shut-upness: not to smother children and totally cut them off from reality but to provide them with a sense of both security and freedom. Sufficient freedom must be allowed and encouraged so that the child can explore and move out into the world and the future with self-confidence. The sense of security is nonetheless accomplished by repressing truths about the child's self and about reality. A child simply cannot bear the full weight of reality. If parents constrain children too much, however, they will succeed only in inflicting their anxieties upon their children and cutting them off from too much reality. Ideal parents shut off their children's world just enough to allow them to explore the world with security and equanimity.

Shut-upness, whether in its healthy forms or in its unhealthy forms, is, to use Becker's terms, a vital lie. Kierkegaard writes, "It is easy to see that shut-upness *eo ipso* signifies a lie, or, if you prefer, untruth. But untruth is precisely unfreedom." [8] These untruths cut us off from reality and possibility and hence freedom. But without them we could not live. The best we can hope for is that our parents have not massively deluded us about the nature of reality, wrapping us in unduly thick protective layers of character that restrict us from moving about adequately in the world of possibility. Our parents must help us make the world manageable without improperly restricting our freedom. In making the world manageable, they are helping to construct the lie that is our self.

One of the dominant forms of shut-upness that Kierkegaard unmasks is exemplified in the character type he calls "the Philistine." The Philistine is the middle- or upper-middle-class person who has been lulled into a sense of security by trivialities. He is protected from knowledge of his true self and the world by his dull, daily routines. To use contemporary terms, the Philistine works at a job he doesn't like, comes home to his wife and two children, reads the paper (pri-

---

8. Kierkegaard, *Concept of Dread*, 114-15, cited in Becker, *Denial of Death*, 72.

marily the sports pages), eats his supper, watches television, and then goes to sleep. On Saturdays, he mows the lawn, watches a baseball game, and plays cards with friends. On Sundays, he gets dressed up for church, sleeps through the sermon, eats a large dinner, takes a long nap, watches some television. On Monday, he is back at work.

The Philistine is proud of his new car, nice home, attractive wife, and well-behaved children. He feels secure and believes that he has obtained the best that life has to offer. Though the Philistine thinks himself free, Kierkegaard contends that he is a slave to cultural expectation and habit. He recognizes his self only by superficial externals. He will live out his days believing that he is both free and happy when he is actually drugged by trivial habit. Kierkegaard writes, "Devoid of imagination, as the Philistine always is, he lives in a certain trivial province of experience as to how things go, what is possible, what usually occurs. . . . Philistinism tranquilizes itself in the trivial."[9]

The Philistine stays in his comfortable world, believing himself to be master of his universe, lord of his castle, and most of all, free. In reality he has cut himself off from vast tracts of reality, embraced unfreedom, and failed to see his authentic self. The social conventions that direct his life and give him his sense of security have created his prison. Were he self-conscious about his life, he would prefer to be tranquilized by the trivial and to remain safely and securely in his own prison than to remain aware of his naked self and the hostile universe.

I will not pursue Kierkegaard's fascinating analyses of other character types — those who shut themselves up even more than the Philistine or those who allow too much reality into their consciousness without the normal and healthy character defenses. Kierkegaard contends that all character, whether healthy or unhealthy, is our way of closing ourselves off from reality. We are led to wonder what reality would be like if we chose not to shut ourselves off from it. How would

9. Kierkegaard, *Sickness Unto Death*, 184-87, cited in Becker, *Denial of Death*, 74.

we then view our self? The central question is this: What would life be like *if we did not lie?* How can we, as mature adults, confront our self honestly in this vast world? We have seen what shut-upness is like: it protects us from perceiving our insignificance. We now need to consider what it means to be an honest, authentic human being.

Kierkegaard believes that authentic human beings are those who see themselves as they really are and who transcend the self that has been so carefully constructed and nurtured since infancy. But to see ourselves without recourse to our character defenses or societal roles is to see that, on our own, we are nothing. To comprehend our genuine insignificance leads to *anxiety.* Stripped of our elaborate attempts at self-justification, we stand alone, unprotected, finite, impotent, mortal, mere creatures. We may be honest, but we are now terrified by our true and insignificant place in the cosmos.

It is easy to see why people, when faced with this knowledge of their true self, retreat to the prison of deceitful character and carefully circumscribed lives. Better to gain the illusory value of having the nicest garden on the block or sending two children to Harvard than to come face-to-face with who, without the lies, we really are. Time to watch more television. "So what do you think of them Cubbies?" The comfortable and trivial entice us back from the precipice of despair. But to return to a Philistine life, once one has stared despair in the face, requires massive self-deception. It requires persuading one's self that, despite evidence to the contrary, one's trivial life really does amount to something deep, abiding, and significant.

It is also easy to see why people who are honest about their self and place in the universe contemplate suicide. They find themselves unable to return to the trivial life of the Philistine. For them, the only relief from anxiety is suicide. Tolstoy, the great Russian writer, found himself in precisely this precarious position. He had written great novels, acquired fame and fortune, lived on a vast estate with many servants at his beck and call, yet he was forced to come face-to-face with his unworthiness and insignificance. Unable to find comfort in

150

the trivialities of his carefully managed and manicured life, he increasingly despaired of any relief save suicide. Although he tried for years to continue to find satisfaction in his earthly comforts and worldly fortunes, honesty forced his despair:

> The deception of the joys of life which formerly allayed my terror of the dragon now no longer deceived me. No matter how often I may be told, "You cannot understand the meaning of life so do not think about it, but live," I can no longer do it: I have already done it too long. I cannot now help seeing night and day going round and bringing me to death. That is all I see. . . . The two drops of honey which diverted my eyes from the cruel truth longer than the rest: my love of family, and of writing — art as I called it — were no longer sweet to me.[10]

Anxiety can drive us back to comfortable self-deception or forward to despair and even death.

Kierkegaard isn't concerned with anxiety as an end in itself; he doesn't delight in despair. Rather, he sees anxiety as a "school" for the development of honest character and genuine human maturity. Anxiety is the means whereby we destroy the vital lie of character. We are left with nothing except our true and unprotected self. We cannot acquire an authentic human life without dying to our constructed self: "the self must be broken in order to become a self."[11]

Anxiety schools us in authentic existence by preparing us to relate to a power beyond the self. Anxiety instructs us in faith. We reject the finite and false sources of power that animate our lives, our character and roles, and replace them with faith in God, the true source of life-giving power. Faith opens up the possibilities of being

10. Leo Tolstoy, *My Confession*, trans. Alymer Maude (London: Oxford University Press, 1940), 20.

11. Kierkegaard, *Sickness Unto Death*, 199, cited in Becker, *Denial of Death*, 88.

connected to a genuinely powerful source of meaning and value. Once we are tutored in despair, we can embrace the true source of power — God — and we can rest in him, knowing that we are merely creatures. Once we recognize that we are creatures and not creators, we are relieved of the impossible task of creating a self.

We need to recognize and accept that our creatureliness is meaningful in relation to a creator. Only by relating to our creator can we acquire cosmic worth. Only by giving up the merely cultural, personal, and necessarily finite and perishing means of acquiring value can we relate to the source of infinite value.

Authentic self-knowledge and the recovery of a meaningful life can occur only with the recognition of the awful poverty of our constructed self and the humble recognition of the self as creature before God. Our haughty, consuming ego is a burden that must be discarded before genuine existence can take place. Our most potent enemy is our self-centered ego, masquerading as a tyrannical king, which requires human victims for its magnification. The king must die. As Becker says in his summary of Kierkegaard:

> Man breaks through the bounds of merely cultural heroism; he destroys the character lie that had him perform as a hero in the everyday social scheme of things; and by doing so he opens himself up to infinity, to the possibility of cosmic heroism, to the very service of God. His life thereby acquires ultimate value in place of merely social and cultural, historical value. He links his secret inner self, his authentic talent, his deepest feelings of uniqueness, his inner yearning for absolute significance, to the very ground of creation.[12]

Faith is the courage to face the dread of our existence as mere creatures, without the lie of character, to die to our constructed self, and to be embraced by the creative power of God.

12. Becker, *Denial of Death*, 91.

Unmasking the self is, as T. S. Eliot writes, "the way wherein there is no ecstasy." We are most likely to recognize our impoverished selves when our constructed defenses prove insufficient to cope with reality — when, for instance, we lose a job or a spouse or a child, when we go through a divorce, or when we approach mid-life and feel that we have accomplished nothing. The moment of recognition may indeed be a moment when our true self is revealed instantaneously. But more likely the "moment" will be a lifelong process where the scab of self is slowly and painfully peeled off. Faith, writes Kierkegaard, is a project for a lifetime.

the chief virtue: humility

It is only when we realize that on our own we are nothing, that we can open our self up to God. The sheer vastness of space and time humbles us. Our puny and trivial attempts to fill up that space with meaning amount to precisely nothing. We must renounce all of our claims to self-righteousness. We must confess that on our own we have nothing that counts. As it says in the old hymn, "Nothing in my hands I bring." In pride we have repeated the primordial sin — "Ye shall be as gods." The unmasking of the self reveals the folly of our presumption and manifests our humiliation.

If pride is the chief sin, then humility is the chief virtue. What humility is may be gleaned from what it is not. It is not attempting to achieve self-worth at the expense of others; it is not being an active participant in the competition of life; it is not being resentful or envious of the accomplishments of others; it is not gossiping about others in an attempt to diminish them and to elevate one's self; it is not being secretly delighted when misfortune falls upon another. Note that I do not contrast humility with self-confidence, self-esteem, or healthy ambition; it is not the denial of these. It is, as Robert Roberts writes, a necessary precondition of all meaningful human fellowships:

153

Humility is the ability, without prejudice to one's self-esteem, to admit one's inferiority, in this or that respect, to another. And it is the ability, without increment to one's self-esteem or prejudice to the quality of one's relationship with another, to remark one's superiority, in this or that respect, to another. As such, humility is a psychological principle of independence from others and a necessary ground of genuine fellowship with them, an emotional independence of one's judgments concerning how one ranks vis-à-vis other human beings.[13]

Humility involves removing oneself from the race of life. If I give up seeing others as competitors for the scarce commodity of glory, I can treat them as equals and can begin to relate to them as friends instead of enemies. Pride leads me to scorn or envy the accomplishments of others; humility allows me to delight in them. Pride forces me to cheer secretly at the pain of others; humility makes me weep at their pain. Only when my joy in their joys and my sorrow in their sorrows is genuine have I become their friend. Treating others cannibalistically, as food for the increase of my self, prevents the creation of friendship. Love is possible only when humility paves the way.

Humility is necessary for the establishment of a proper relationship with God. Only when we give up the project of creating our self at the expense of others — of ceasing to be god — can we relate in faith to God. Only then is our self-esteem firmly established in the honor that God freely bestows upon us, an honor or a valuing that cannot be lost. Our deepest desire — for significance — finds satisfaction in the esteem of God.

A great parable of humility can be seen in the life of John Merrick, in the film *The Elephant Man*. Merrick was afflicted with a horrible disease that disfigured his entire body and face. His hair was falling out;

---

13. Robert C. Roberts, *Spirituality and Human Emotion* (Grand Rapids: Eerdmans, 1982), 62.

his head was the size of a beach ball, with protruding grotesque tumors; his back was a field of grizzled growths; he was unable to walk or breathe properly. He seemed to his contemporaries best suited to be a sideshow freak. They didn't recognized the human in him but called him "it," "thing," "freak," "animal," "monster." He was paraded in front of gawking crowds who paid money to see him. Deprived of adequate food and shelter, often beaten, treated no better than an animal, he was forced to perform humiliating acts against his will and for the enjoyment of his civilized "betters." In the climax of the movie, Merrick is chased by a crowd of men who mistakenly believe that he has assaulted a small girl. They finally corner him in a public bathroom. Instead of striking back and confirming their opinion that he is no better than an animal, he screams: "I am not an animal! I am not an animal! I am a human being!" In a touching final scene Merrick claims that, in spite of his sufferings, he has had a happy life. He exclaims: "I am happy every hour of the day. My life is full because I know that I am loved." Stripped of the typical defenses of "normal" life, Merrick is forced to depend upon God in ways deeper than most of us could understand. His voice is first heard earlier in the film reciting Psalm 23. His deep faith in God enables him to persist in the human project despite being cruelly afflicted. His acceptance of life as a gift empowers him to view life as a manifestation of divine goodness and mercy. In spite of the horrible circumstances of his life, he takes in joy and love and new experiences like a child. He has an openness to the world, to friendship, and to love that makes him victor and not victim. At bottom is a deep humility that allows him to cling not to health, wealth, or looks but to divine mercy for his strength of character and his source of self.

finding my self

When the demigod is dislodged and the tyrant is renounced, the self is reestablished through faith in God. What God takes away with his left hand, he gives back again with his right. In faith, says Kierkegaard, the pupil of possibility gains infinity. We find our identity grounded in the infinite, eternal, and creative God who can fill our otherwise petty lives with significant value. Only when our desire to be number one is vanquished can we see our self as it truly is and then, in faith, enjoy being supremely valued by God.

Only in God's love and acceptance of us, not in our puny human accomplishments, can we find our self-worth.

God does not know us as white, male, racist, or famous. God knows us by name. He has written our names on the palm of his hand and he will not forget us (Isaiah 49:16). He knows us and esteems us; in that is our abiding source of self. We still wish to be valued, and faith finds that wish satisfied by the esteem of God.

> When I look at your heavens, the
>   work of your fingers,
>   the moon and the stars that you
>   have established;
> what are human beings that you
>   are mindful of them,
>   mortals that you care for
>   them?
>
> Yet you have made them a little
>   lower than God,
>   and crowned them with glory
>   and honor.
>
> Psalm 8:3-5

Who we are — creatures esteemed by God — is vastly more valuable than what we do.

If we dispense with all finite sources of value and desire, in humility, to find our self-worth in the Infinite Source of value, then we must take on the Infinite's scheme of values. We must renounce our narcissistic reliance on fashionable clothing, youthful vigor, physical attractiveness, wealth, power, and fame. We must abandon our racism, sexism, elitism, religious exclusivism, and nationalism. We must remove all the props that falsely elevate us above others. We will not find our true self in the gym, in front of the mirror, on the front page of the newspaper, or at a political rally. We find our true self on our knees. We must affirm that the goal of human existence is not to win at the expense of others but to become the kind of person we were designed to be. We were designed to love and enjoy each other, the creation, and God. We are created to desire happiness, and we will find our true happiness only in fellowship, not competition, with one another and with God. As Augustine writes, "Thou hast made us for Thyself and our hearts are restless until they rest in Thee." God wants us to quit the race of life and to enjoy his Sabbath rest.

Resting in the esteem of God does not mean removing ourselves from life. We return to family and friends and to labor and leisure. But instead of *using* family and friends and fame as means to self-glorification, we *accept them as gifts to be valued and enjoyed in themselves.* Resting in God goads us into actively participating in and enjoying life in all of its possibilities. What does the Lord require of us? That we do justice, love mercy, and walk humbly before our God (Micah 6:8). Resting in the esteem of God means valuing and esteeming other people, in meaningful and lasting relationships, as God values and esteems us.

Although the foundation of our self-esteem is the honor granted us by God for who we are and not for what we do, we can enjoy that honor in tangible ways. Instead of garnering begrudging praise in *competition* with others, we can enjoy generous affirmation in *fellowship* with them. We can participate in the divine act of conferring honor through kind words and deeds. The spontaneous proclamation of one another's value can spread the honor that God has freely bestowed upon us. Genuine human affection, liberally imparted, is central to God's redemptive work in the world.

two stones

There are two improper responses to this chapter. One would be to wallow in self-pity at the realization of our insignificance. "I am a worm." On our own, left to our feeble human conventions, we cannot invest our lives with the kind of significance we so desperately desire, but God can. God's esteem can fill to the brim our empty cup of self and give us lasting value and meaning. I have tried in this chapter not simply to tear down, but to tear down in order to build up — this time on the foundation of God's esteem of us, not on the puny foundation of the esteem of others. Some people have already had the stuffing knocked out of them; their self-esteem should not plunge any lower. Those who already feel that their lives are empty of meaning need to experience their lives invested with the esteem of God.

Another improper response would be to allow the possession of religious truths to puff one up with pride. Religious belief that becomes an occasion for feeling superior to the "non-elect," the "reprobate," is a cultural artifact, a human construction to prop up the feeble self once again. It is pride masquerading as devotion. This sort of belief must be dismantled. Those of us tempted toward religious pride need to see the poverty of our self apart from the esteem of God and to accept God's esteem in humility.

What is the proper response to these challenging but liberating truths? Let me conclude with some advice from the Hasidic teacher, Rabbi Bunam: "A man should carry two stones in his pocket. On one should be inscribed, 'I am but dust and ashes.' On the other, 'For my sake was the world created.' And he should use each stone as he needs it."

158

chapter 10

Stages on
Life's Way

What I really lack is to be clear in my mind *what I am to do*, not what I am to know, except in so far as a certain understanding must precede every action. The thing is to understand myself, to see what God really wishes *me* to do; the thing is to find a truth which is true *for me*, to find *the idea for which I can live and die*. What would be the use of discovering so-called objective truth, of working through all the systems of philosophy and of being able, if required, to review them all and show up the inconsistencies of each system; — what good would it do me to be able to develop a theory of the state and combine all the details into a single whole, and so construct a world in which I did not live, but only held up to the view of others; — what good would it do me to be able to explain the meaning of Christianity if it had *no* deeper significance *for me and for my life;* — what good would it do me if truth stood before me, cold and naked, not caring whether I recognized her or not, and producing in me a shudder of fear rather than a trusting devotion? I certainly do not deny that I still recognize an imperative of understanding and that through it one can work upon men, but it must be taken up into my life, and that is what I now recognize as the most important thing.

Kierkegaard, The Journals

ooooo

We have already learned from Kierkegaard something about becoming an authentic self. We have seen that living authentically, honestly, and self-consciously means rejecting the pride of creating our self and accepting with humility the gift of God's esteem.

160

It means accepting our self and life as gifts. And the first step toward accepting and enjoying these gifts is to acknowledge that we have lost our true self beneath our clothing—our roles, our judgments, our ethnic heritage, and our social status. Attaining to authentic selfhood requires courage—to stand apart from social conventions and familial expectations, to stand alone before God and in faith accept who we are, to accept responsibility for choosing our own destiny, and to open our selves up to possibility. In this chapter I want to explore further how we may become authentic individuals—true selves—by digging a bit deeper into the thought of Kierkegaard. In particular, I want to focus on his description of the stages on life's way, that is, the steps in the process of seeking and finding our true selves. To do this, I think it will be useful to begin by sketching just a bit of the historical context of Kierkegaard's life and thought.

background

Kierkegaard (1813-1855) lived in mid-nineteenth-century Denmark, where the church was state-sponsored and supported. Being born a Danish citizen entitled one to be an official member of the state church. There was little difference between being a citizen and being a Christian. In a typically sarcastic tone, he writes:

> Among the many and various things which man needs on a civilized plane and which the state tries to provide for its citizens as cheaply and comfortably as possible—among these various things, like public security, water, lighting, roads, bridge-building, etc., etc., there is also . . . an eternal blessedness in the hereafter, a requirement which the state ought also to satisfy (how generous of it!) and that in as cheap and comfortable a way as possible.[1]

1. Søren Kierkegaard, *Attack Upon Christendom*, trans. Walter Lowrie (Princeton: Princeton University Press, 1968), 99.

The state church reduced Christianity to superficial adherence to external formalities, all the while ignoring inward transformation. It had forgotten what inwardness is. The Danish church was a social gathering place where businessmen could show off their finery and lovely wives and smart children, meet other businessmen, go off to lunch, and close a deal. Being a Christian meant little more than the nineteenth-century equivalent of membership in the country club — it was one's civic duty, it could enhance one's business prospects, and it was an opportunity to show off one's social status.

Kierkegaard had a profound distrust of such institutions because they tend to absorb the individual. According to Kierkegaard, one's authentic individuality is measured by how one stands before God, and institutionalized religion often hinders one's relation to God. He despised the sociocultural reduction of Christianity to citizenship. Genuine Christianity is simply a choice to accept or reject God's Word. This is the supreme decision and the core of all human existence. He described his task as a writer: "I am . . . a religious author, . . . the whole of my work as an author is related to Christianity, to the problem 'of becoming a Christian.'"[2]

Kierkegaard was adamantly opposed to the abstract theorizing typical of philosophy in his day. Philosophy had removed itself from life. In his view, philosophy should devote itself to intensely personal reflection on what is most important in life. He sought a philosophy for which he could live or die. He wrote of the passion that should attach itself to the philosophical endeavor, not as a mere intellectual exercise but as a means to proper action. He believed that whatever one is committed to should make a difference in one's life.

Important choices in life, according to Kierkegaard, are criterionless, that is, not dictated by reason. If a choice were dictated by reason, then I would be coerced by reason, and the choice would not be made

---

2. Søren Kierkegaard, *The Point of View for My Work as an Author,* trans. Walter Lowrie (New York: Harper and Row, 1962), 5-6.

by me. My most significant choices should be freely made. If reason does not dictate a choice, then it is *my* choice. Each of the stages on life's way must be entered by free choice. With this background in place, let us now turn to Kierkegaard's discussion of the stages on life's way.

the aesthetic stage

The first stage on life's way, the place from which we all start, is the aesthetic stage. It is the stage in which we are committed to the satisfaction of our own desires, to the saturation with sense experience. Hedonism, crass or sophisticated, is probably the best modern term for this stage. The person in the aesthetic stage acts without constraints and without consideration for the future. The aesthete may know the difference between right and wrong but does not act accordingly. The aesthete lives in and for the moment and fills the now with as much sensation as possible. The aesthete may pursue sex, drugs, and rock and roll; or consume gourmet food and fine wine; or partake of safe sex and high art. The aesthete can be either a grungy rocker or a sophisticated yuppie. Since they pursue the same end — satisfaction of desire — the yuppie and the punker occupy the same moral plane.

The aesthete's pursuit of the sensual is rooted in emptiness. He is driven by desire but, when sated, only desires more. He is filled with hungers that cannot be satisfied. He skitters like a rabbit through life from one pleasure to the next, oblivious to the rapid flow of time that moves him toward destruction, without friendship or love.

The enemies of the aesthetic life are pain and boredom. Pain is the obvious enemy to one who is devoted to pleasure. Pain can roust us out of our exclusive commitment to self; it can force us to consider the world beyond the self. Pain has the peculiar power of pointing out the severe limits of pleasure seeking. The ultimate pain, which

163

devotion to the now prevents the aesthete from seeing, is death. Death cuts the aesthete off from the life-pursuit of persistent self-satisfaction.

The second enemy of the aesthetic stage is boredom. To stave off boredom, the aesthete seeks novelty. Kierkegaard describes this stage as "The Rotation Method." The aesthete may start off drinking beer, but boredom forces a switch to wine and then fortified wine, and then hard liquor, and finally drugs. Or the sexual aesthete starts with a single partner but out of boredom seeks out new and perhaps multiple partners, even perfect strangers, and pursues ever more exotic sources of sexual pleasure.

For a contemporary dramatization of the aesthetic stage, consider addicts of crack cocaine. Crack directly stimulates the pleasure centers of the brain, and the feelings are so intense that people can become addicted with a single trial. That first rush of pleasure is so overwhelming that users will do anything to repeat it. So they ask for more. But the second time is never as good as the first time. So they try even more. But that time is not as good as the first time. Eventually they give up, go home to sleep and then, as darkness falls, attempt to recapture that original high. The first high of the night is the best, but never as good as that first one, and the cycle repeats itself. Junkies call the quest for recapturing that first overpowering sensation of pleasure "chasing the ghost." And junkies will do anything — sell their parent's property, their body, and even their own children — to capture that elusive ghost. The pressure of novelty, just to keep enough pleasure going, forces ever more variety for an unattainable high. It is no wonder that in this case the quest for novelty often leads to death.

Every aesthete is chasing the ghost of a fully satisfied life. We are more than animals, more than bodies, and we cannot attain happiness simply by satisfying our animal desires. Human beings are a unique synthesis of body and soul, the finite and the infinite, the temporal and the eternal, the free and the necessary. The authentic person creatively engages all of the parts of human nature. The aesthete,

164

however, focuses upon the bodily, finite, and temporal side of human nature and ignores the other parts. The impoverished spirit of the aesthete asserts itself in uneasiness, melancholy, and despair. Increased novelty may stave off boredom for a while and delude us with a counterfeit happiness, but humans are not constructed to be satisfied simply by the stimulation of their nerve endings.

People stuck in the aesthetic stage believe themselves to be free, but in reality they are bound by their unreflective pursuit of pleasure. Lacking reflectiveness and free choice, their self is lost, hidden beneath and chained by their unconscious desires and social customs. Genuine freedom and authentic selfhood require conscious reflection and liberation of will, both of which are ironically absent in aesthetes, who pride themselves on being the most free of all people. Consider the college student who, with the approval of his friends, drinks heavily, sleeps late every day, skips as many classes as possible, picks up a different woman at the bar each weekend. He thinks he is free, but he is really a slave to the pressure of his peers and his desires. He avoids self-conscious reflection on his self and life, so his true self remains an enigma to him. The self disappears in a crowd of friends. The aesthete has forgotten what it means to exist and knows nothing of that "restlessness and striving, and fear and trembling, which should obtain for the entire life."[3]

The enemies of the aesthetic stage, pain and boredom, have the potential to drive the aesthete to self-reflection, to separate him from the fleeting present and connect him imaginatively to the past and the future, to time and eternity, from necessity to possibility.

Pain and boredom can lead the aesthete to the threshold of despair over the emptiness of a life devoted to pleasure. Beyond that threshold lies the ethical stage.

3. Søren Kierkegaard, *Journals and Papers,* ed. Howard and Edna Hong (Bloomington: Indiana University Press, 1967), 77.

the ethical stage

The ethical stage is entered into and sustained by self-conscious choice. In the act of deliberately choosing, the ethical person sets himself or herself apart from the crowd and begins the process of becoming an individual, a true self. Although the self has been fashioned in part by one's environment, instincts, passions, inclinations, and desires, the ethical person assumes responsibility for that self and self-consciously chooses not to be determined by social and physical conditions. The ethical person is free to fashion the self, within limits, according to a choice for the good. The person at the ethical stage is self-conscious both of his socially and physically imposed self and of the ideal self towards which he is striving. Only when one is aware of but not limited by one's conditioned character may one freely choose to rise above the given self and become one's ideal self.

The first step along this path is the decision not to be an automaton programmed by desire, habit, and social custom. Freedom from the necessity imposed by these restraints opens the self up to possibility — to what one ought to be. In the aesthetic stage, one revels in what one is — selfish, pleasure-seeking, uncommitted. In the ethical stage, the ideal beckons one beyond what one is to the way one ought to be. Goodness attracts the ethical person away from selfishness and towards duty.

The ethical stage is the sphere of duty, of universal rules, of unconditional demands and tasks. At the ethical stage, one not only strives toward the universal but incorporates the universal into one's own life. The goal is both out there guiding us and inside animating us to walk that path. Kierkegaard writes that the ethical person "has his teleology in himself, has inner teleology, is himself his teleology. His self is thus the goal toward which he strives."[4] The Kingdom of God is within.

---

4. Søren Kierkegaard, *Either/Or*, vol. 2, trans. Walter Lowrie (Princeton: Princeton University Press, 1944), 279.

Although the aesthete may do his duty to satisfy his selfish desires, the ethical person feels the weight of duty itself and has the passion to incorporate the universal into himself. The ethical individual is not thereby absorbed into the universal; rather, each individual becomes a unique expression of the universal. According to Kierkegaard,

> Duty is the universal which is required of me; so if I am not the universal, I am unable to perform my duty. On the other hand, my duty is the particular, something for me alone, and yet it is duty and hence the universal. Here personality is displayed in its highest validity. It is not lawless, neither does it make laws for itself, for the definition of duty holds good; but the personality reveals itself as the unity of the universal and the particular.[5]

The universal unites in the individual in the self's unique relations in life and work; the self finds itself in relationship to others. This is expressed in one's vocation or calling, which is each person's particular expression of the universally human and the individual. Creative work and self-sacrificial relationships join to lift one above the aesthete's mundane world of desire and custom into the meaningful world of the universally human. The ethical part of our nature, which the aesthete represses or ignores, is expressed in our significant labors and proper loves. And the self, which the aesthete was compelled to conceal, is revealed to others and to us in love and friendship. Human love and creativity were made to find satisfaction in beings and things beyond the self; exclusive devotion to the self subverts the proper satisfaction of our deepest longings. Our life and work produce a profound sense of community that makes us feel at home and that vanquishes our desperate feelings of being strangers in this world.

But what if, try as we might, we cannot heed the call of duty when the universal beckons? The ethical stage, according to Kierkegaard,

---

5. Kierkegaard, *Either/Or*, vol. 2, 268.

"is that of requirement, and this requirement is so infinite that the individual always goes bankrupt."[6] The enemy of the ethical stage is guilt. And guilt leads to despair. The ethical life ends with St. Paul's lament: "For I do not do the good that I want, but the evil I do not want is what I do. . . . Wretched man that I am! Who will rescue me from this body of death?" (Rom. 7:19, 24).

If guilt engenders dissatisfaction in the ethical stage, then one may out of despair take a leap of faith into the next stage, the religious stage. But the costs of such a leap are great and the leap is not dictated by reason. So one may return to the ethical stage, hoping against hope that one can repress one's sense of guilt and shame as one's sense of duty increases. But the more earnest one is about one's duties, the more one's sense of guilt must increase. So the bankruptcy of the ethical life may prompt one to take the leap of faith into the religious stage.

the religious stage

In *Fear and Trembling* Kierkegaard describes the transition from the ethical to the religious by considering the figure of Abraham. In demanding that Abraham sacrifice Isaac, God demands something that, from the standpoint of the ethical, is absolutely forbidden, a transgression of duty. Abraham must take a leap of faith. He must suspend the ethical. No rules can guide this choice — it is criterion-less. God fiercely demands absolute obedience of Abraham — to leave family, friends, and country and to sacrifice his only beloved, Isaac. From the standpoint of the ethical, this is ludicrous. The religious calls for the suspension of the ethical. From the perspective of reason and ethics, we cannot be sure that we are not wrong. If we know

6. Søren Kierkegaard, *Stages on Life's Way*, trans. Walter Lowrie (New York: Shocken Books, 1967), 430.

anything at all, we know that fathers ought not kill their sons. But that is precisely what God has called Abraham to do. Both reason and morality call such choices into question; that is why in the religious stage one must work out one's salvation in fear and trembling.

Why make a choice that is, from the standpoint of the aesthetic and the ethical, absurd? Because it is the only way to find one's self. The religious stage marks the highest personal transformation of the self — the self can only be fully actualized in relationship to God; only then does one lose one's dreads as the fear of death and of guilt drop away.

If the enemy of the ethical stage is guilt, then the religious stage involves the admission that one is a sinner. One may remain in the ethical, mired in despair and paralyzed by one's inability to do good, or one may move one out of the realm of the purely ethical into a search for forgiveness. The guilty self requires unconditional love. The search for unconditional love cannot be satisfied by the recognition of more rules, and the search opens the individual up to powers beyond itself. As Kierkegaard writes: "An ethics which disregards sin is a perfectly idle science; but if it asserts sin, it is *eo ipso* well beyond itself."[7] With the aid of the divine, the religious person breaks through the universal to the individual.

The first step of faith in the religious stage is what Kierkegaard calls "infinite resignation": the self dies to the world, freely confesses itself to be finite, renounces the pretension involved in constructing the false self, and acknowledges the power of the absolute. The self acknowledges that it is nothing before God; it sees the great chasm separating sinful human beings from a holy God.

One dies to one's self, but one also rises. The second step of faith is the appropriation of forgiveness. Self-renunciation brings one to the place where "humanly speaking no possibility exists" — where

---

7. Søren Kierkegaard, *Fear and Trembling,* trans. Walter Lowrie (Princeton: Princeton University Press, 1968), 108.

further progress seems, from a finite, temporal, conditioned perspective, impossible. But with God all things are possible and redeemable.

In the religious stage, the disparate paradoxes of our character are united into a meaningful whole. We can feel secure in our finitude if we relate to an infinitude that is ultimately caring. We can accept responsibility for our social conditioning if God grants the power to overcome our conditioning and freely carve our character in terms of our calling. We can avoid the paralysis of our sinful nature if there is forgiveness. We can affirm our bodily nature if it is ruled by our spirit. We can feel unchained from the necessities of time if the eternal breaks into the temporal and redeems wasted time and opportunity. We can be freed from the despair that pain, boredom, and guilt bring to a life dictated by desire or duty. At the religious stage, the necessary and the free, the finite and the infinite, the temporal and the eternal, the sinner and the saint are all kept in creative tension through faith in God.

The religious person is not an insensible ascetic, forever renouncing the pleasures of this world. The religious person is not driven from the ethical and the aesthetic but gets them both back. The religious stage demands the renunciation of the self and misplaced desire, but what God takes away with his left hand he gives back with his right — aesthetic and ethical experience properly expressed. So one returns to the feast of life, but not as one driven by an insatiable appetite for sex, fame, wealth, or honor. Rather, one accepts and enjoys all things — adequate food, shelter, and clothing; sex and its pleasures; personal recognition; financial reward; earthly honors — as the gifts they are but not as sources of identity or self-worth. The pupil of possibility, as you recall, gains infinity.

Life is an adventure, and religious persons have opened themselves to possibility. The fastidiously ethical person is plagued by the fear that he might do something wrong. As Aristotle argued, there is only one way to go right but an infinite number of ways to go wrong; the chance of hitting that narrow mark of goodness is precious thin.

So the ethical person may be paralyzed by fear of wrongdoing. But the religious person is liberated from the tyranny of fear and guilt. He is motivated by the encouragement of the possible, not by fear of doing something wrong. He moves boldly into his calling, accepting the risks that life presents.

God calls us out of the doldrums of our drugged lives into the world of unlimited possibility. In that wide world, freed from the chains of social expectation and desire and from the fear of moral failure, we devote ourselves to the very service of God. Affirming our unique calling — to stand alone as individuals in obedience to God — we find our authentic self.

The process of faith, of self-actualization through self-denial, is not accomplished in the blink of an eye. Faith is a project for a lifetime. Authentic selfhood, Kierkegaard writes, cannot be gained in a half hour's lecture but requires the effort of a lifetime: "To understand this requires fear and trembling, silent solitude, and a long interval of time."[8]

the way

This discussion of the liberation of the true self through the death of the ego has relied chiefly on Christian symbols and terms, but transcending the self is universally affirmed by the major religions of the world. The major religions differ on the goal of salvation, but the process is often strikingly similar: the ego must die because it impedes relating to something greater than the self, which is required for liberation or salvation. It cuts us off from God, Nirvana, unity with Brahman, bliss, others, and our authentic self. Unless we can transcend the ego, we are trapped within our self-composed limitations. My account of these religions is necessarily brief and sketchy, but it

8. Kierkegaard, *Point of View*, 8.

illustrates the universally attested wisdom of transcending the ego. I shall briefly consider representative versions of Buddhism, Hinduism, Judaism, and Islam.

According to Buddhism, in order to attain bliss, one must lose all sense of personal identity; the self must be extinguished. The Tao, or the Way, is to eliminate the self. Consider the following dialogue between a Buddhist master and a pupil:

> What is the Tao?
> It is right before your eyes.
> So why can't I see it?
> Because you have a Me.[9]

The self is liberated, according to Buddhism, when it ceases to desire even the desire to exist. Nirvana occurs when one is freed from desire and moves into the Void, nothingness.

Hinduism, in some of its branches, is more gnostic than moral and focuses on certain dualisms that are nothing more than illusions. Reality is One and needs to be recognized as such. The self, in contrast to others or the Other, is an illusion that must be overcome. Hinduism contends that one is not led toward the Void but rather toward the discovery of the highest truth that Brahman or Atman is everything and is One. If Brahman is everything, then I am Brahman and not some other distinct self. Oneness with Brahman, therefore, requires the death of the ego. According to the Hindu saint Ramakrishna, Kali, the Divine Mother, assists in the death both of selfishness and the self in the attainment of oneness with Brahman: "If it so pleases Her, She takes away the last trace of ego from created beings and merges it into the consciousness of the Absolute, the undifferentiated Godhead. Through Her grace the finite ego loses

---

9. Quoted in Frederick Franck, *The Book of Angelus Silesius* (New York: Knopf, 1976), 21.

itself in the illimitable Ego — Atman — Brahman."[10] Only when the distinct self is eliminated may one attain the silent bliss of oneness with Brahman; in so doing, one shares the eternality and purity of Brahman and is thereby liberated from both death and guilt.

Religions like Buddhism tend to see salvation or human fulfillment in terms of the self being absorbed into the undifferentiated All or Nothing, while Western monotheistic religions typically see the new self as continuing into a life of worship and praise of God. In either case, however, the independently derived self is the enemy of salvation and must be destroyed before one can attain happiness, Nirvana, or the *visio Dei.*

Judaism is a covenant religion specifying rights and responsibilities of the respective parties. The Hebrew covenant is based on the two unequal partner's willingness to assume their proper roles: "I will be your God and you will be my people." Since the primordial sin is pride — "Ye shall be as gods," in the serpent's words to Eve — the removal of the usurping self from the divine throne is the first step in acceding to the covenant. The early Hebrews seemed to understand salvation primarily in political and temporal terms. Later Hebrew writings shift the discussion towards an afterlife in the shadowy realm of Sheol. In the Psalms and the prophetic writings, however, there is a deep sense of the need for salvation both from self and sin and from death.

Sufism's tolerant and mystical interpretation is often considered the heart of Islam. According to Sufism, the purpose of external religious observances like praying, fasting, tithing, pilgrimage, and worship is to effect an internal transformation. Various exercises are devised by the Sufi masters in order to deflate the ego and establish in the individual the supremacy of Allah. In order to be united with God, one must give up everything that is of this passing world, in-

10. *The Gospel of Sri Ramakrishna*, trans. Swami Nikhilananda, abridged ed. (New York: Ramakrishna-Vivekananda Center, 1974), 12.

173

cluding the self. Al-Junayd, drawing on the Koran, believes that the self must be annihilated, that there must be a cessation of being. The self must be denied before it can be united with the One.[11] The greatest of the Sufi masters, Rumi, illustrates this point:

> A disciple seeking the Sufi path finally feels he has mastered it and arrives to announce this to his master. He knocks on the door and when asked "Who is there?" answers "I." The master says, "Go away, you have not yet acquired knowledge." He leaves to return after he has performed more spiritual exercises, and this time when asked who is knocking says "Thou." "Come in," says the master. "There is no room for two I's in this house."[12]

Union with God requires abandoning both one's self and the mundane world.

The preening ego is universally perceived as an obstacle to union with God, ultimate reality, one's authentic self, and others. The world's religions hold up renunciation or annihilation of the self as a remedy for humanity's deepest malady. I don't mean to claim that all religions exemplify the full Kierkegaardian conception of the religious stage. Some religions, for example, seem content to take the first step in the religious stage, infinite resignation, without proceeding toward recovery of one's authentic, individual existence in relationship with the eternal. Nonetheless, all of the great world religions are united in affirming that the overweening self is the primary obstacle on our path to human happiness, authentic existence, salvation, or enlightenment.

11. Frederick Matthewson Denny, *An Introduction to Islam* (New York: Macmillan, 1985), 257.

12. Quoted in Akbar S. Ahmed, *Living Islam* (New York: Facts on File, 1994), 56.

chapter 11

Home

Why does our earliest childhood always seem so soft and full of light? A kid's got plenty of troubles, quite unarmed against pain and illness. Childhood and old age should be the two greatest trials of mankind. But that very sense of powerlessness is the mainspring of a child's joy. He just leaves it all to his mother, you see. Present, past, future — his whole life is caught up in one look, and that look is a smile. Well, lad, if only they'd let us have our way, the church might have given men that supreme comfort. Of course they'd each have had their own worries to grapple with just the same. Hunger, thirst, poverty, jealousy — we'd never be able to pocket the devil once and for all, you may be sure. But man would have known he was the son of God; and therein lies your miracle. He'd have lived, he'd have died with that idea in his noodle — and not just a notion picked up in books either — oh, no! Because we'd have made that idea the basis of everything: habits and customs, relaxation and pleasure, down to the very simplest needs. What we would have got rid of, what we would have torn from the very heart of Adam, is that sense of his own loneliness.

Georges Bernanos, *Diary of a Country Priest*

Fly, envious Time, till thou run out thy race:
Call on the lazy leaden-stepping Hours,
Whose speed is but the heavy plummet's pace;
And glut thyself with what thy womb devours,
Which is no more than what is false and vain,
And merely mortal dross;
So little is our loss,
So little is thy gain!
For, when as each thing bad thou hast entombed,
And, last of all, thy greedy self consumed,
Then long Eternity shall greet our bliss

With an individual kiss;
And Joy shall overtake us as a flood,
When every thing that is sincerely good
And perfectly divine,
With Truth, and Peace, and Love, shall ever shine
About the supreme throne
Of him, to whose happy-making sight alone
When once our heavenly-guided soul shall climb,
Then, all this earthy grossness quit,
Attired with stars we shall for ever sit,
Triumphing over Death, and Chance, and thee, O
Time!

John Milton, *On Time*

ooooo

Many Christians believe, without being able to say why, that God gives life meaning. They believe that the problem of death is conquered by their belief in life after death. But the problems of life are not solved simply by living *longer* (who, after all, desires an infinite extension of their current life?). A wretched existence is best terminated, not extended indefinitely. Answers to the problem of the meaning of life must ensure that we will live *better* and that we will find life satisfying and meaningful. Indeed, eternity will have to be so satisfying that we avoid boredom forever! How does God satisfy our desire for a rich and full life?

We have already seen that God honors us, satisfying our need for self-esteem. Knowing this liberates us from the tyranny of self-will and allows us the freedom to be creatures instead of creators. We have also seen that God's unconditional love satisfies our desire for forgiveness and releases us from the fear of guilt and death. In this chapter we will explore two final themes: the need for a home and the need to redeem time. Home is a metaphor for a variety of concerns: for security, warmth, peace; for the need to feel that the world is not ultimately hostile to our plans and prospects; for the belief that our journeys are not in vain but have a goal. We also want to seize the time, to fill it with meaningful and worthy activities, but we have squandered precious time, and it is in increasingly short supply. We cannot get time back. Can time be redeemed?

going nowhere

What does the world look like from the perspective of one who denies the existence of God? The atheist rejects the Christian view of the universe — that it is providentially governed by a fundamentally good and personal being who is concerned for the welfare of his creatures. The atheist believes rather that the universe is ruled by blind and accidental forces that make no special provision for human welfare or conduct. The fundamental structure of the universe is neither moral nor personal; it is simply there. Human creatures are only cosmic accidents, chance conglomerations of atoms, whose existence is not necessary, purposeful, or significant. Our sojourn on earth is desperately brief, and then we are trundled into the ground. The final words are death and destruction.

In one of the most famous and eloquent statements of atheism in the twentieth century, Bertrand Russell describes the world of which I speak:

Such in outline, but even more purposeless, more void of meaning, is the world which science presents for our belief. Amid such a world, if anywhere, our ideals henceforward must find a home. That man is the product of causes which had no prevision of the end they were achieving; that his origin, his growth, his hopes and fears, his loves and his beliefs, are but the outcome of accidental collocations of atoms; that no fire, no heroism, no intensity of thought and feeling, can preserve an individual life beyond the grave; that all the labors of the ages, all the devotion, all the inspiration, all the noonday brightness of human genius, are destined to extinction in the vast death of the solar system, and that the whole temple of man's achievement must inevitably be buried beneath the debris of a universe in ruins — all these things, if not quite beyond dispute, are yet so nearly certain that no philosophy which rejects them can hope to stand. Only within the scaffolding of these truths, only on the firm foundation of unyielding despair, can the soul's habitation henceforth be safely built.[1]

This is the human predicament as the atheist views the world — life without the consolation of the eternal. What does the perspective and possibility of the eternal bring to human life? In Russell's view the goal of human life is death and nothingness; everything we hope for, aspire to, and accomplish is doomed to dissolution. We will become nothing forever. Our deepest desires cannot, according to this view, be satisfied; our fondest hopes are beyond realization; our most cherished accomplishments are destined to be forgotten, if not now, then tomorrow.

Jean-Paul Sartre likewise affirmed the inevitable frustration of all human endeavor. Human actions, according to Sartre, project into the

1. Bertrand Russell, *Why I Am Not a Christian* (New York: Simon and Schuster, 1957), 106-7.

future. Human beings set goals for themselves that are, ultimately and fundamentally, future oriented. We hope for security, peace, and happiness and try to realize those hopes. Our deepest hopes transcend the present moment. Yet our hopes are dashed by the realization that our fundamental goals cannot be attained. Human reality, Sartre believed, is essentially a failure. Since there is no divine providence holding out the promise of redemption, no next life in which our fondest hopes are realized, the human condition is one of inevitable and undeniable despair.

Beneath our despair is our sense of abandonment by God. Sartre writes: "When we speak of 'abandonment' . . . we only mean to say that God does not exist, . . . and man is in consequence forlorn, for he cannot find anything to depend upon either within or outside himself."[2] Abandonment is not merely the lack of faith in God but a profound sense of spiritual lostness, emptiness, contingency, and aloneness. We no longer feel that the universe is our home.

> What is man that the electron should be mindful of him? Man is but a foundling in the cosmos, abandoned by the forces that created him. Unparented, unassisted and undirected by omniscience or benevolent authority, he must fend for himself, and with the aid of his own limited intelligence find his way about in an indifferent universe.[3]

The despair of a godless world haunts Albert Camus as well:

> What, then, is that incalculable feeling that deprives the mind of the sleep necessary to life? A world that can be explained even with bad reasons is a familiar world. But, on the other hand, in a universe

2. Jean-Paul Sartre, *Existentialism and Humanism,* trans. Philip Mairet (London: Methuen, 1946), 32-34.
3. Sartre, *Existentialism and Humanism,* 32-34.

suddenly divested of illusions and lights, man feels an alien, a stranger. His exile is without remedy since he is deprived of the memory of a lost home or the hope of a promised land. This divorce between man and his life, the actor and his setting, is properly the feeling of absurdity.[4]

If we are not headed toward a goal, if there is no terminus for our existence, no ultimate and attainable purpose for our strife and striving, then the world is an absurd place. If we believe that we are not headed for our true home and that there is no goal that will make ultimate sense of life, then we must agree with Russell, Sartre, and Camus that the world is absurd.

Imagine a war which neither side has any chance of winning; all they can do is fight, without the prospect of ultimate victory. There might be minor successes here and there, but, in the end, no one wins. The fight simply carries on interminably. If you were in this war and became aware of your plight, you would surely feel the battle absurd. I suppose we might feel better if we could delude ourselves into thinking that we were winning and would win the war. But Russell, Sartre, and Camus ask us to look at life without illusions and lights — to see that life is a battle that can't be won, a journey to nowhere.

going home

My son Will has a blessed ignorance of the travails of life. When he was a toddler, he would wake in the middle of the night cold and scared. His imagination filled the room with dragons, snakes, and nasty shadows. Invariably he would get up and leave his room. I would hear him open his door and then close it (he would always close it behind

---

4. Albert Camus, *The Myth of Sisyphus and Other Essays,* trans. Justin O'Brien (New York: Knopf, 1958), 6.

him, maybe to keep the bad guys inside). By the time he was astride our bed, I would hold open the blankets and invite him in. Wrapping my arms around his trembling body, I would kiss him, whisper "I love you," and assure him that everything was all right. Surrounded by the warmth and security of his parent, he would quickly drop off to sleep. I dread the day when Will is too old to climb into my bed when frightened, to sit in my lap when perplexed, or to run into my arms when sad or in need of affection. But now as an adult, I too want the warmth and security of sitting in my father's lap and knowing that everything is all right. But my father is dead, and I am too old to sit in laps, anyway. Rather than find the security I need, I stand alone.

God, our heavenly Father, seeks the intimate relationship of parent to child. When we feel alone, afraid, and overwhelmed, God wants us to walk into his room, shut the door behind us, and to embrace us in the warmth and security of his love. God wants me to trust him as my son trusts me.

In Georges Bernanos's *Diary of a Country Priest,* there is a discussion of the meaning of Christianity. An old, worldly wise priest tells the country priest of the title, "The opposite of a Christian people is a people grown sad and old."[5] Reflective non-Christians feel misplaced, lonely, even superfluous. Christians, on the other hand, believe that they are children of God. The priest sadly comments, however, that we have lost our sense of divine comfort. If the church had done things right, he says, "what we would have got rid of, what we would have torn from the very heart of Adam, is that sense of his own loneliness."[6]

The old priest describes the boredom and lostness of a humanity "come of age." We are technological giants, yet moral midgets. We can split the atom, but we don't know why we are here. We have put our faith in the power of science but find it too weak to answer our

5. Georges Bernanos, *Diary of a Country Priest,* trans. Pamela Morris (London: John Lane, 1948), 27.
6. Bernanos, *Diary of a Country Priest,* 27-28.

deepest questions of human existence. As science advances, our place in the cosmos becomes more uncertain. We have "lost the soul of [our] childhood." What we need, and what science cannot provide, is joy in a sad world, the smile of God to animate our lives.

To the eye of faith, the world is not a strange place for even stranger creatures. It is the setting for our journey home. "Softly and tenderly, Jesus is calling . . . calling, O sinner, 'Come home.'" What helps us through the dinginess and suffering of this life is the belief that we have a home. Having a home means that the journey of life has a destination, that we are not headed nowhere, that our moral and spiritual struggles are not for naught.

Our earthly homes should provide a glimpse of the divine home; they should be places of security, trust, openness, and compassion. We should strive to make them microcosms of our divine home. The Church too should be a welcoming community of broken but compassionate people. It should provide a place of rest from the race of life. A respite on our way to our Sabbath rest.

absurdity or hope?

Camus's analysis of absurdity centers on our loss of a home. We desire to live at peace and forever, to have a place that we can call home. The realities of this world, though, thwart these desires; they will wreck, for all eternity, our home. Our deepest desire bumps into the reality of the world and, according to Camus, the godless world conquers. We feel like strangers, alienated from the world. Human beings are a poor fit for the slots of this world.

Absurdity, according to Camus, results from a bad fit between our deepest desires and the realities of this world. The situation is only slightly improved for the Christian. From cradle to grave, the world is still absurd. Even if we do things right, there is no reason to believe that we will be happy. Even if our lives are without blemish, we may not avoid depression. The Bible itself warns of the poor fit between us and the world: "Blessed are those who are persecuted for the sake of righteousness." In this life, wickedness is sometimes rewarded and righteousness is sometimes punished. The world is often a threat. People are in competition. Love and justice are scarce commodities. Camus's response to this incongruity is to revolt against it — to deny that it is part of some divine plan.

We need to embrace Camus's passionate struggle against the absurdity of this world; we need to fight with all our might against the darkness. The world, after all, is fallen — it is bent and contorted and we with it. We no longer fit properly, and the twisted world dooms our twisted life plans. Camus revolts against the frustrating world, with no prevision of ultimate success. We need to revolt, but with *hope*. We can live genuinely satisfying lives only if we give up the notion that life is *ultimately* absurd. For Camus, absurdity is the final word, to which the only reply is revolt. For the Christian, absurdity is only penultimate; the final word is reconciliation. Christians believe that all suffering will be redeemed, that justice will triumph, that human beings can be recreated in the image of God, and that the world will be transformed into a place fit for the image bearers of the divine. Christians see their lives as part of a redemptive process — to struggle against darkness and to transform it into light. Camus has a deep understanding of the fall; what he lacks is any hope of redemption.

If all that I have written about living an authentic, meaningful life is true, why are non-Christians often happy and Christians often in despair? Non-Christians are able to attain some measure of happiness because grace is imparted in many human activities: enjoying a fine meal, appreciating lovely music, losing oneself in a game or hobby or a good book, taking a walk in the woods, engaging in meaningful labors, sharing moments of self-disclosure with a soul mate, connecting emotionally and spiritually with one's spouse, returning to childhood with one's children. Any activity that liberates us from our ego can deeply satisfy any human being. But these are only glimpses of the joy that God intends for his creatures. We often mistake these signs for the reality they signify. They are intended to point us to a deeper satisfaction and higher happiness.

So why aren't all Christians happy, fulfilled, living satisfied and meaningful lives? The world is still a bad fit for human beings and is still in need of redemption. Christians have a foot firmly planted in both worlds — the city of God and the city of the world. We have minds that are mixed both in belief and in practice. While we desire fellowship with God and pursue righteousness, we also doubt, fall short, and retain our commitments to the world. Our twin allegiances ensure that we will find peace and joy — find our home in the midst of worldly concern — only fleetingly in this life.

redeeming time

I just wasted forty-five minutes waiting for my doctor. I could have spent that time with my children, but it is lost to me now. If only I could figure out how to manage my time better, I wouldn't be sitting here marking time, trying not to read the *Sports Illustrated* swimsuit issue, but devoting my time to moral and spiritual growth, family, vocation, or culture. Perhaps I could devise some way to get my doctor to do some time for all the time he's made me wait over the years.

We waste time, spend time, mark time, pass time, spend quality time, buy time, do time, organize time, manage time, lose time, and make up for lost time. When we are children, time is unending and death is unreal. But we age all too rapidly, and time speeds up like a boxcar careening out of control. We've got to get it under control, but we can't. Our life project of moral and spiritual development is pressing in on us, and we are running out of time.

T. S. Eliot's remarkable *Four Quartets* reminds us of the frailty and furtiveness of time and of our need for redemption from it. As he travels on London's subway, he studies the faces of his fellow travelers through time. Puffed up with exaggerated self-importance, they are plunged into the dim world of the London underground. Here, in the darkness, their lostness is illuminated.

> . . . Only a flicker
> Over the strained time-ridden faces
> Distracted from distraction by distraction
> Filled with fancies and empty of meaning
> Tumid apathy with no concentration
> Men and bits of paper, whirled by the cold wind
> That blows before and after time. . . .[7]

How much of our time spent is mere distraction? Are we filled with fancies but empty of meaning? Which of our actions and accomplishments really count on our journey of life? Are we making progress or is our life a frantic series of missed opportunities? How can we redeem time? We redeem people, culture, families, and the world. Can we also redeem time?

Perhaps time is finite, bounded on one side by birth and on the other by death. In the fleeting middle, we cram our lives with all that we can fit into them. Our lives move through time like a meteor passing through the cosmos. We give off a bright flickering light, full of the promise of a shimmering future. Our past wags behind us like a glittering tail. But the more distance covered, the longer the vacuous tail grows. We become all past, and our future dims to a dot. We hit the earth's foul atmosphere of disease, dissolution, and death, and with one last flicker, we die and disappear. And we hope against hope that we will leave our mark on this earth, that our crater, our passing, will be vast and deep.

Or maybe our lives have a beginning in time but meld finally into

7. T. S. Eliot, *Four Quartets* (London: Faber & Faber, 1944), 10-11.

eternity with God. Our lives move through time like a drop of water from the top of a mountain to the sea. In the precipitous fall we accelerate rapidly towards our destination. Along the way we pass through enchanted meadows and alongside grotesque factories. We wend our way through precipitation and pollution. As we turn this way and then that, we take into ourselves a little or a lot of the beauty, bilge, and bile we scrape against on our constraining shores. We grow larger, change in color, get thicker, gain more speed, and then, drop by drop, we are swallowed up in the vast ocean.

The Christian view is that we don't get smaller as we get older; we get bigger. We are in the process of becoming creatures of heavenly delight or hellish derision. Our every choice feeds our inner self and either enriches or impoverishes it. Our choices within this time are the merest beginnings of our eternal quest.

I remember sitting in my parents' living room just a few days after the death of my father. I looked at his chair and remembered him sitting there, watching a basketball game or just napping in his favorite flannel shirt and blue jeans. Then I remembered his habit of flossing his teeth in that chair just before going to bed. I chuckled as I recalled how much that used to infuriate my mother. And then I was struck with the odd thought: Why floss your teeth if you know you are going to die? Why spend your time on that sort of activity if it is finally of such little consequence? Why jog, lift weights, diet, watch your cholesterol, and coddle your hair when you know no matter what you are doomed. In short, why do we focus so much of our time and attention developing those parts of ourselves that in the end are shucked off like husks of corn?

My father grew up in a large and poor family from which he was eventually turned out into an orphanage. He left high school for the Korean War and returned to college, marriage, and three kids in quick succession. He rose early to haul garbage to support his family while he was in college. He was devoted to his children and spent most of his free time carting us from one activity to another. He worked long and thankless hours pioneering a program in the inner city of Kalamazoo that provided poor families with recreation, education, and nutrition. He sacrificed so his children could go through life more easily than he did. Scarred but unbowed, my father learned self-sacrifice, generosity, good humor, long-suffering, and forgiveness. He may have lost his teeth, but he gained his soul.

Things like weight loss, prevention of baldness, and wrinkle-free skin are, indeed, goods. Let us call such superficial goods "light-values" (or, as contemporary advertisers might put it, ValueLite). But patience and self-sacrifice are enduring and deep goods. Let us call them "heavy-values." Christians pursue glory *(doxa)*, which literally means "weight." Some of our glory is gained simply by virtue of being image bearers of the divine. Because of the Fall, however, that image needs to be restored through human responses to divine grace. We need to regain the weight of glory that was lost through our diet of iniquity. Virtuous moral and spiritual choices fill our souls with nutritious food. The heavy-values prepare us for eternity — they are values that cannot be lost. The prevention of baldness may last a lifetime, but self-sacrifice endures forever.

Heavy-values connect our time with eternity. We gain heavy-value within time because of our relation with an eternal being. We pursue heavy-values to nourish our souls for eternity. But we have moral anorexia — try as we might to put on heavy-values, we are starving ourselves by sneaking the junk food of light-values. If we are to succeed, God must enter into and redeem time. But time creates its own problems — even an omnipotent being cannot change the past. What's done is done and cannot be redone, even by God. God cannot make Adam and Eve not to have sinned. Once one is unchaste, God cannot make one a virgin.

Since God cannot change what has been done, there is only forgiveness. And for that, God had to enter into time. The pollution, bilge, and bile of our lives must be removed. We are not fit to enter into the ocean of the divine. So the divine must enter into the river

188

of time to help make us fit. To redeem time, God must enter into time. God has to dip his feet into the streams of our lives. As Eliot writes, "Only through time time is conquered."[8]

still and still moving

> Old men ought to be explorers
> Here and there does not matter
> We must be still and still moving
> Into another intensity
> For a further union, a deeper communion. . . .[9]

So writes T. S. Eliot in his profound poetic discussion of Christian belief and life, *The Four Quartets*. We must be still and still moving.

We must be still. We can rest in the comfort of knowing and trusting in the Lord of the universe. "Be still and know that I am God." There is a moral and spiritual center of the universe, and around that center our lives revolve. At the center of the universe is not an impersonal "It" dictated by a blind and fatal concourse of events but a personal "Thou" — a benevolent and wise creator and sustainer whose plans and purposes we may trust. We must be still in that knowledge. Our trust in God will falter at times. We are no more perfect in faith than we are in life. Yet the line has been drawn, and we have stepped over onto the side of Christ. We have taken the decisive first steps of faith, and now we are moving toward the light. We must be still.

We must be still and still moving. While our lives our centered in Christ, his redemptive work demands that our lives keep moving. We are pilgrims, explorers on a journey to find our true home. We

8. Eliot, *Four Quartets*, 10.
9. Eliot, *Four Quartets*, 22-23.

scarcely see how far the journey will carry us. There are others to love, places to see, and children to raise. There are people to be served, books to be read, and chores to be done. We have been paddling about in the shallows, and now it is time that we begin the plunge into deeper waters. We must be still and still moving.

We must see our time on earth as an arena for moral and spiritual development. We must never become complacent, never feel that we have arrived. When I graduated from college, I was foolish enough to think that I had grasped nearly every important truth there was to know about God and myself. But this pretension has been progressively unmasked. When I was in graduate school, my father would invite me to walk with him in his garden. He would tell me how well his peas were doing and how ripe the melons were. I would feign interest, unable to comprehend how he could be so concerned with peas and melons. I was too busy with important things to be bothered with broccoli and beans. I was winning souls in Young Life and arguing about the existence of God in graduate school. I could not be bothered with something so lowly and mundane as a garden. I lacked the moral maturity to discern the sheer joy that my father experienced in being connected to the growth, life, death, and rebirth of natural things. I had failed to learn that working with the hands is just as noble as working with the mind — that it is good for the soul to let one's hands mix with the dirt. And most of all I lacked the sensitivity to discern that my father was offering me a gift — of gardener's wisdom and fresh fruit and, most of all, himself.

We must be still and still moving. We must live knowing that God is perfecting the good work that he has begun in us and that he will bring it to completion. We must take the pilgrimage of life as the adventure that it is — as we work and play, travel and travail, read good books and climb high mountains, have our babies and bury our dead. Never satisfied, we must be still and still moving into another intensity, a further union, a deeper communion.